Jewels in the Crown

RAY HUTTON

Jewels in the Crown

How Tata of India transformed
Britain's Jaguar and Land Rover

First published 2013 by Elliott and Thompson Limited
27 John Street, London WC1N 2BX
www.eandtbooks.com

ISBN: 978-1-908739-82-7

1 3 5 7 9 10 8 6 4 2

A CIP catalogue record for this book is available from the British Library.

Typeset in Baskerville by MacGuru Ltd
Printed and bound in the UK by TJ International Ltd

Contents

Introduction

WHEN TATA OF INDIA bought Jaguar and Land Rover from the Ford Motor Company in 2008, most people on the car side of the motor industry didn't know much about Tata Motors. While other motor companies had taken advantage of India's manufacturing base to supply low-cost small cars for world markets, Tata didn't export many of its own cars. It was to make a much grander entrance to the world stage by acquiring two of the most famous names in motoring, the jewels in the crown of the British motor industry.

That crown was somewhat tarnished. There had been several decades of decline in car manufacturing in the UK. Jaguar, which had made the most sought-after sports cars in the world and proved their worth by winning the Le Mans 24 Hours race year after year, had fallen behind the times and wasn't engaging with the new audience for premium cars. Land Rover was known for making the best four-wheel drive vehicles but was threatened by campaigns to make big, heavy sport utility vehicles (SUVs) socially unacceptable. And both Jaguar and Land Rover had patchy reputations for reliability.

Tata determined to build on the illustrious heritage and worldwide recognition of these brands. It faced plenty of scepticism but in less than five years Tata had silenced all the doubters: Jaguar Land Rover (JLR) moved from loss to substantial profit; it had become the world's fastest-growing premium car company, and one of the most successful in terms of return on revenue. Jaguar Land Rover's investment is the biggest in the UK motor industry in 50 years.

This book is an account of how this impressive business turnround was achieved. Jaguar Land Rover exists to make cars, so the story follows the concept, design and development of its products, the methods of production, and how they are promoted and sold across the world. To understand the heritage, it must also look back to the automotive icons that Tata inherited: the Jaguar E-Type and XJ6, the original Land Rover, and the Range Rover, king of the SUVs.

A motor manufacturer is a powerful mix of finance, engineering and marketing. The key to any industrial turnround is management, so this is also a story of people. Until recently, most of the world's motor industry was run by a close-knit group of 'car guys' who didn't welcome outsiders. Such are the convoluted histories of Jaguar and Land Rover that many senior managers have worked for one or both brands, separately or together, and, in some cases, several times.

In broad terms (as there have been any number of changes in company names and brand style), Jaguar has had four owners in the 68 years since it was formed from SS Cars and Land Rover has changed hands six times since its first vehicle appeared in 1948.

Each of the previous owners left some mark on the ways that Jaguar and Land Rover are regarded today. The early chapters are brief histories of the two marques and how they developed. In the 1960s they were brought together in what became British Leyland, then went their different ways, to be reunited as part of Ford's Premier Automotive Group in 2000.

Ford's changing circumstances, and personnel, are described in some detail to explain the lead-up to and conduct of the sale. And the background to Tata shows how it emerged from being an outsider in the bidding contest to drive a hard bargain and become the proud and ambitious owner of the two famous brands.

It also shows that one man was the driving force behind the deal and subsequent developments: Ratan Tata, chairman of the eponymous Group, who reached retirement age as the fifth anniversary of the takeover approached and this book was being written.

As well as being an industrial history, this is an allegory of the motor business over half a century: the decline of the British motor industry and the loss of the private companies operating within it; consolidation and foreign ownership; difficulties for mass-producers and the rise of premium brands; and the centre of gravity of sales shifting to Asia, predominately China.

As a long-serving writer and commentator on the car business, working for media in the UK, the US and India, I have been following the fortunes of Jaguar and Land Rover since the British Leyland era. My work has also taken me to the Indian car industry and Tata Motors, before, and since, the Jaguar Land Rover acquisition.

The Appendix includes a cast list of key figures in the evolution of Jaguar and Land Rover and the company's current structure. I have met and talked with all but two of those listed and most of the other motor industry personalities included in this book. Where they are quoted directly, it is from interviews, on-the-record meetings which I attended, and previously published material.

There are still others, not mentioned by name, who were most helpful in guiding me through some of the more contentious aspects of Jaguar's and Land Rover's past and recent activities. I thank them for their forbearance and apologise to them and to you, the reader, for any errors or misinterpretations as, except where noted and quoted, the analysis and views expressed are my own.

Ray Hutton
London, March 2013

Author's Note

OF NECESSITY, there is some duplication of facts and happenings across chapters as the history is built up from three different directions and the recent development of each brand is treated separately. Although they are integrated as never before, Jaguar Land Rover strives to maintain a distinct individual character and voice for each brand.

The reader may also be confused by financial information being given variously in US dollars and pounds sterling. Essential figures are given only in the currency used at the time of the transaction or in published financial results. If these were quoted in the two currencies at any given time, the fluctuating £/$ exchange rate (ranging from 1:1 to 1:2 over 30 years) could make comparisons with earlier or later figures meaningless.

Jewels in the Crown

1

'A car company of consequence'

RATAN TATA AND RAVI KANT sat at one end of a square of tables in a packed room at the Villa Sarasin, an elegant fin-de-siècle mansion once located in extensive grounds but now hidden by the concrete expanse of Palexpo, the Geneva exhibition centre.

The chairman and managing director of Tata Motors were no strangers to the Geneva Motor Show and its attendant press corps. The Indian company had exhibited the Indica, its first family car, in 1998, when it generated only mild interest from financial journalists and the other motor manufacturers who use the show preview days as an annual business convention.

Earlier that day, 4 March 2008, Tata had held its normal press conference on the motor show stand – a brief speech introducing its latest models, which included the Nano, the back-to-basics 1-lakh (100,000 rupees, £1,250) car that was expected to revolutionise the still-evolving Indian car market. But the untypically large crowd of journalists and photographers was there for another reason. They wanted, needed, to get a glimpse of and a comment from the bosses of the Indian company that was about to become the owner of two of Britain's most revered car marques – Jaguar and Land Rover.

The Ford Motor Company had declared Tata the preferred bidder for its crown jewels just two months earlier. Newspapers and radio and TV stations swamped the company with applications for interviews with the chairman, Ratan Tata. To meet all those requests was impossible, so Tata Motors communications chief, Debasis Ray, arranged a round-table conference for a selected few, off-site at the Villa Sarasin.

Ratan Tata, courteous and softly spoken, explained that Tata was deep in due diligence at Jaguar and Land Rover and had yet to reach agreement with Ford – that would take another three weeks – so he could only talk of hopes and expectations, not solid plans. But he left no doubt about his company's ambitions:

> Ten years ago we came to the Geneva Motor Show as a new car company trying to find a place in the global motor industry. Tata is trying to become a car company of consequence.
>
> Jaguar and Land Rover are iconic brands that we respect enormously. These companies were for sale. We were invited to bid and were pleased to be considered. We were not on the prowl to acquire another car company. This is a great opportunity; a few years ago one would not have thought these brands would be available.

Several of his inquisitors broached, directly or indirectly, the issues that were debated by car enthusiasts and motor industry pundits around the world: what does a company making cheap cars for India, with a poor record of quality and reliability, know about making high-technology and high-performance premium cars? Will Tata move production to India, with its lower cost base, and take Land Rover technology to improve its own more rudimentary four-wheel drive vehicles? And if Ford – one of the world's biggest motor manufacturers – can't make money from Jaguar and Land Rover, how will Tata succeed? Ratan Tata was reassuring:

> We would retain the image, touch, and feel of Jaguar and Land Rover, not tinker with the brands in any way. Our philosophy for any companies we become involved with, is that we grow with them, take them forward. Our interest in Jaguar and Land Rover is not based on outsourcing, or taking their technology. Our challenge will be to nurture the brands and make them thrive.

In the UK, where curry is now regarded as a national dish, the press had been full of snappy headlines about the 'Indian takeaway' of Jaguar and Land Rover. Ratan Tata was asked if customers would accept traditional British cars from an Indian-owned company, and, by a representative of the more liberal-minded media, whether this was in some way a strike against the memory of British colonialism.

Tata already owned some 18 businesses in the UK, including Tetley Tea, a leading provider of the national beverage, and only a year before had paid £6.7 billion to take over Corus, the Anglo-Dutch steel firm. Ratan Tata, who has run the Tata Group according to British corporate principles, could see no problem in Indian ownership of Jaguar and Land Rover:

Many people, I imagine, did not know that Ford of America had owned Jaguar and Land Rover for many years. We are very conscious that the brands belong to Britain and they will continue to be British. Who owns them is not as material as the brands themselves, the enterprise and the people.

In all the companies we acquire, we have to be satisfied that they share the same value systems and ethical practices and that we gel on a human level.

So this is not a special moment for me in the sense of a developing country taking over in the old world. Anyway, I was well under-age when the Raj ended...

Journalists and commentators, invariably a cynical group, came away from this Geneva encounter feeling far more positive than most had expected. Elsewhere, financial and industry analysts pointed to the smooth transition at Corus and concluded that Tata would be a good custodian for these two famous but wearied British car brands.

Tata finalised the agreement with Ford to buy Jaguar and Land Rover on 27 March 2008. The price was $2.3 billion. The sale was completed on 2 June. Tata Motors, the fourth-biggest truck and bus manufacturer in the world and the first Indian engineering company to be listed on the New York Stock Exchange, was on its way to becoming 'a car company of consequence'.

2

Jaguar's faded glory

WILLIAM LYONS was the last of the patrician motor moguls. When he retired as chairman of Jaguar in 1972, he had run the company for nearly 50 years. It had grown out of the Swallow Sidecar Company, which he had established with a partner in Blackpool and progressed to coach-building stylish bodies for Austin Sevens, Standards and Wolseleys, and caddish, long-bonneted SS sports cars.

The business moved to Coventry in 1928, repaired aircraft and made components during the Second World War, and, fearful of SS being associated with defeated Nazi Germany, changed its name to Jaguar Cars as soon as the war was over, in 1945.

The new Jaguars became known for their sleek appearance, high performance and value for money. Lyons was the company's driving force, involved with every aspect of the cars' development and production, particularly their design, for which he had a sharp, discerning eye. His special talent was to create cars that were both pleasing aesthetically and aspirational: a sure-fire marketing proposition for a glossy, optimistic post-war world.

Success came with the XK120 sports car from 1949, a beauty that could do more than 120 mph when few production cars could reach 100, and led to a series of racing sports cars that were to win the Le Mans 24 Hour race five times in the 1950s and, in 1961, to the legendary E-Type, a 150 mph car sold for less than half the price of anything with the same performance.

The Jaguar saloon cars of the same period – the 2.4, 3.4 and 3.8 – are remembered now through films and TV as the cars of choice for both villains and the police flying squad but historically are more important for showing the way to the compact sports saloons that were to make BMW the supreme premium car maker in the twenty-first century.

Lyons, who was knighted in 1956, was an autocrat. Although Jaguar was a public company, he held a majority of the shares and made most of the decisions without reference to his fellow directors. According to one source,[*] there were no board meetings until the mid 1960s.

He had bought Daimler, the British car and bus manufacturer, in 1960, followed by Guy Motors, a commercial vehicle maker, and Coventry Climax, an engine specialist that was dominant in Formula 1 motor racing. But the 1960s were difficult times for the British motor industry, which was beset with labour problems, declining markets and increasing development costs. In 1965, the British Motor Corporation (BMC) – which included Austin, Morris, Riley and Wolseley cars – bought Pressed Steel, the company that made Jaguar car bodies.

---

[*] Ken Clayton, *Jaguar: Rebirth of a Legend* (London: Century, 1988).

In 1966, Lyons, approaching retirement age, began to be concerned about succession, for which he had made no provision, and Jaguar's position in the changing industrial scene. With Pressed Steel, rival BMC controlled the supply of its cars' most essential components. Lyons proposed a merger between BMC, Jaguar and Pressed Steel. It became British Motor Holdings (BMH). BMC chairman, Sir George Harriman, was the chairman of the new company but Lyons retained the title of chairman of Jaguar, and his business remained largely autonomous.

BMH didn't last long. The Labour government, intent on improving the efficiency of British industry, encouraged cooperation with Leyland, a truck and bus maker that had recently acquired Standard-Triumph and Rover. That resulted in the formation, in 1968, of the British Leyland Motor Corporation (BLMC), which was the beginning of the end for Lyons as a motor magnate (in 1972, aged 70, he was given the honorary position of president of Jaguar) and, coincidentally, the first time that Jaguar and Land Rover came together in the same company.

The management of BLMC, which changed with monotonous regularity, struggled to handle Jaguar. There was no love lost between the engineers at Rover, Triumph and Jaguar and there was uproar when the factory in Browns Lane, Coventry, occupied by Jaguar since 1951, was renamed 'Leyland Cars Large Car Assembly Plant'. Those who were put in charge of the Jaguar division – for that is what it had become – had limited freedom of action and lacked Lyons' intuition for attractive, saleable cars.

This was a critical period for Jaguar, which reached a production peak of 31,549 cars in 1971 and continued to make an annual profit of around £5 million, although it was now part of a huge group that was losing money unsustainably. Classic car enthusiasts regard the E-Type as the icon but actually it was the 1968 XJ6 that defined Jaguar for the years to come. Sports and grand touring cars came and went but the core of the Jaguar range was the lithe, fast but comfortable XJ saloon.

By 1975, BLMC was broke and the British government, which saw it as 'too big to fail', reluctantly took it into public ownership. It was a time of industrial strife, from which British Leyland, Leyland Cars and BL, as it was progressively renamed, never really recovered.

Jaguar foundered as part of the JRT (Jaguar Rover Triumph) sub-division but Margaret Thatcher's Conservative government, which came to power in 1979, had begun moves to return BL to the private sector, starting with Land Rover and Jaguar. Land Rover was consistently profitable and easier to separate from the Leyland jungle because Jaguar was not self-contained – and had perpetual trouble with the quality of bodies and paintwork supplied by the former Pressed Steel plant at Castle Bromwich.

At the same time, it was recognised that, if it was to thrive – and eventually separate as a viable business – Jaguar needed more autonomy. As a first step, Castle Bromwich would be put under its control.

In 1980, John Egan, a forthright Lancastrian, was appointed chairman of Jaguar Cars Ltd and was promised a free hand to run the business. He inherited a company beset with industrial unrest and dire quality problems which had halved sales demand: 9,200 employees were making just 14,000 cars a year and the company losses amounted to nearly £50 million a year.

Egan's first message to the employees was: 'We have to turn this round, otherwise Jaguar will be closed.' He has subsequently admitted that closure came 'very close' but step-by-step he addressed the problems – reducing the workforce, settling labour disputes, improving quality and productivity, getting tough with suppliers that produced second-rate components – and returned Jaguar to profitability.

Egan put his stamp on Jaguar, the first person to do so since Sir William Lyons, with whom he formed a cordial relationship. Lyons was proud to see the company he founded being taken back into private ownership in 1984, the year before he died at the age of 83.

There were flirtations with Ford, General Motors and BMW but the British government wanted a stock market flotation, rather than selling one of its prized assets to a foreign company. To guard against an unwelcome takeover bid, it would retain a 'golden share' to expire in 1990. The stock market offering was made in August 1984, with a price of 165p. It was eight times oversubscribed. Jaguar was once more in private hands.

Jaguar was to have less than six years as a stand-alone company. It was successful initially, launching the long-delayed (and government-funded) new XJ saloon, code-named XJ40, and new engines and open-topped versions to revive flagging sales of the XJ-S sports model. It increased brand awareness with an ambitious racing programme on both sides of the Atlantic.

In 1986 it was geared up to produce 40,000 cars a year, and made a very respectable profit: £83.4 million from revenue of £830.4 million. Exports to the United States accounted for more than 40 per cent of sales.

In retrospect, it is clear that Jaguar became too dependent on transatlantic exports. Fluctuating exchange rates made selling in the US an uncertain business and were the main reason for Leyland pulling MG out of America. So while Jaguar reached record production of 49,500 in 1988, as the pound strengthened and the US dollar declined, its earnings started to deteriorate. The situation was made worse by the return of quality problems with the new version of the XJ6.

Egan realised that Jaguar was a minnow in the ocean of the world car industry and that, for a small manufacturer of premium cars, the cost of new model development was disproportionately high. Jaguar had increased its engineering headcount and paid £50 million for the former Chrysler UK technical centre at Whitley, near Coventry, but Egan feared that it might not have sufficient financial strength to meet future requirements.

He began to look around for partners, bigger companies that could reduce these ever-increasing costs, and favoured a proposition from General Motors whereby it would take 30 per cent of Jaguar and share components and technology with Opel and Vauxhall. But while that was being discussed, Ford came along with a killer bid to buy the whole company. It offered £8.50 a share, amounting to £1.6 billion.

That was in October 1989 and the British government's 'golden share' was still valid. Jaguar's directors had to recommend the Ford bid to the shareholders but it was far from certain that the government would allow it. But Ford knew that it was owed a favour. Four years before, Margaret Thatcher had approached Ford about buying Rover and Land Rover – and Bob Lutz, then chairman of Ford of Europe, was keen – but her invitation was withdrawn in the wake of the controversial 'Westland Affair', the furore surrounding the sale of Britain's last helicopter company. She would not allow Ford to be rebuffed again.

Ford paid a high price, considering that Jaguar was losing money at that point and that Ford had not been able to carry out any due diligence. When it did get inside, it calculated that Jaguar's tangible assets amounted to just £300 million. The story may be apocryphal, but when Ford's dour chairman, Red Poling, challenged John Egan for selling him a £300 million company for £1.6 billion, the Jaguar chairman is said to have replied: 'When you go to a fancy restaurant you go for the steak and the sizzle. You have paid £300 million for the steak and

£1.3 billion for the sizzle.' Nine years later, at the launch of the Jaguar S-Type, Poling's successor, Alex Trotman (who had been one of the negotiators), remarked: 'Everything I know about shareholder value I learned from John Egan.'

Ford, the original blue-collar motor manufacturer, wanted a fancy car company. It already had a share of Aston Martin, acquired on the whim of Henry Ford II, who was fond of the finer things in European life, but Aston was a boutique, making a few hundred cars a year. Ford management in Dearborn, Michigan, identified the need for a car that customers could move up to, beyond Lincoln, its US premium brand.

The premium car market was growing. Mercedes and BMW enjoyed the status of luxury goods in the United States and the Japanese car firms, at the height of their powers as mass-producers, had just launched their upmarket contenders – Acura (Honda), Infiniti (Nissan) and Lexus (Toyota).

Ford's communications officers briefed journalists about the rationale of the Jaguar purchase and the aims and strategy for its development. Then, as now, BMW was its role model. Jaguar's two-model range (XJ and XJ-S) would be expanded with new cars to compete against BMW's best-selling 3 and 5 series. Ford confidently expected that, within a few years, Jaguar's output would grow from 50,000 to 200,000 cars a year.

Meanwhile, Egan backed out, his task completed, and Ford sent in Bill Hayden, its British manufacturing chief, to be Jaguar chief executive. The blunt-speaking Hayden was horrified by what he found at Browns Lane and Castle Bromwich. He said that the worn-out facilities and working conditions and procedures were the worst he had seen in any plant 'apart from Gorky' (in Russia). At that later S-Type event, Alex Trotman quipped: 'There was nothing wrong with Jaguar manufacturing that a bulldozer couldn't fix.'

Hayden applied Ford manufacturing principles to Jaguar. He held back new products until he could see the results of modernising, setting higher quality standards, and cutting costs by improving efficiency. And he curtailed projects that seemed unlikely to produce a decent return – like XJ41, the long-awaited F-Type that was supposed to be the authentic successor to the E-Type.

Hayden retired after three years at Jaguar and was succeeded by Nick Scheele, a Briton who had run Ford in Mexico, and a more emollient character with a talent for motivating people. In America, Ford bosses seemed to have dialled back their ambitions for the company. At the chairman's year-end press conference in December 1995, Trotman said: 'Jaguar is doing well; it will make 40,000 cars this year.'

But in the background, the fast-moving Jacques (Jac) Nasser, head of Ford automotive operations and soon to follow Trotman as chief executive, was planning an altogether bigger future for Jaguar. There were to be two new models, both sharing their chassis platforms and mechanical parts with higher-volume Ford models.

The first of the new-deal Jaguars would be the S-Type, introduced in 1998, and built on the DEW98 rear-wheel drive platform designed in the US for a new small Lincoln, the LS. The second, which appeared three years later, was the X-Type, based on a European Ford Mondeo adapted with four-wheel drive.

This caused disquiet inside and outside the company. Could these cars maintain the character of a Jaguar? Wouldn't the brand be diluted by using parts from cheaper, more commonplace cars?

Nasser, a Jaguar enthusiast, was adamant that it would lose nothing and had everything to gain. For the S-Type and Lincoln LS, which shared 60 per cent of components, engineers from

Dearborn and Coventry worked side-by-side. A chassis engineer from Jaguar said: 'Don't think of a dumbed-down Jaguar, just a much better Lincoln.' When it was launched as a smaller and less expensive companion to the XJ, the S-Type was generally well accepted, although the 'neoclassic' styling by Jaguar design chief, Geoff Lawson, received mixed reviews and there was criticism of some plastic interior fitments that were clearly more Ford than Jaguar.

But if Jaguar's loyal customers gave the S-Type a cautious welcome, they were less generous to the X-Type, even though it resembled a shrunken XJ. Everyone knew that underneath the body was a Mondeo and in this case the Jaguar engineers had been able to do no more than tinker with an existing chassis. Jaguar learned some hard lessons here, which it must continue to heed.

Nasser and Scheele continually emphasised Jaguar's Britishness while simultaneously using a veiled threat of making its new models somewhere else in the Ford empire to extract the maximum in UK government grants and assistance. It received £72 million to establish a new S-Type production line at the Castle Bromwich factory and £42 million to take the X-Type to the former Ford Escort plant at Halewood, near Liverpool and save it from closure.

With these new models, together with the XK8 coupe and convertible, which had been launched in 1996, the original long-term sales target looked possible. But, by then, Jaguar was once again incorporated within a bigger enterprise.

In March 2000, as BMW announced that it was giving up its six-year tenure of the Rover Group, Nasser swooped in on Land Rover with a £1.85 billion bid that was almost equivalent to the sum that BMW was having to write off to dispose of the business. The previous year he had recruited Wolfgang Reitzle, a former

BMW high-flyer, and put him in charge of the newly created Premier Automotive Group (PAG), which encompassed all Ford's high-end brands: then, Jaguar, Volvo, Lincoln and Aston Martin. Now Land Rover was added. It marked both a change of scale and attitude. Nasser's target for PAG before Land Rover was 1 million cars a year by 2004. Jaguar was supposed to contribute 200,000 but the arrival of Land Rover meant that that number was less critical, as he foresaw that the two brands could share many resources.

Synergies between Jaguar and Land Rover were to be central to PAG's development. The two brands had been under the same ownership before but there had been no direct connections, or sharing of systems and components. So this is where the story of Jaguar Land Rover, as we know it today, really begins. But in 2000 no one could have guessed where it would be in 2008.

3

Land Rover – cars for all reasons

LAND ROVER grew out of the Second World War. It is no secret that the original vehicle was inspired by the US Army Jeep but its creation had more to do with Britain's economic and industrial situation in the late 1940s.

Rover was a conservative company which had built its first car in 1904. Its advertisements stated, with appropriate modesty, that a Rover was 'One of Britain's fine cars'. In 1945 it emerged from the six years of war, during which its Coventry and Solihull factories had made aero engines and components for aircraft and tanks, with a range of cars that had been designed in the early 1930s.

Government austerity measures restricted the number of cars that it could produce and where they could be sold. Steel supplies were linked to exports but aluminium was unrestricted and readily available, surplus from the aircraft industry. Rover needed a stop-gap to utilise the large Solihull plant until a new generation of saloon cars was ready and a free home market returned.

Land Rover publicity today perpetuates the romantic idea that Spencer and Maurice Wilks, the brothers who ran Rover, drew the first Land Rover with sticks in the sand and that it was knocked up in a workshop using aluminium recycled from wartime aeroplanes. A corporate film makes neat connections to the way today's Defender, the linear descendant of the original Land Rover, is used for hedonistic purposes on tropical beaches and the all-aluminium construction of the 2013 Range Rover.

In reality, the Wilks Brothers had been planning a new small car using Birmabright aluminium alloy, which was produced by a company run by Maurice's neighbour in Birmingham, and the Land Rover was intended as an agricultural vehicle, inspired by the need to replace the four-wheel drive war-surplus Jeep that he used on his farm in Anglesey, North Wales.

The first prototype actually used a redundant Jeep chassis, with the engine and a variety of parts from existing Rover saloons. The final product, with a Rover-designed steel chassis and simple, flat aluminium body panels, made its debut at the Amsterdam Motor Show in 1948 and subsequently was exhibited at agricultural shows up and down Britain.

The Wilks thought that there might be a market for 2,500 Land Rovers a year but at the end of its first 12 months they had sold 8,000. It was not just for farmers; buyers included builders, emergency services, government departments, and individuals based in countries where there were scarcely any roads.

The Land Rover was quickly established as the best vehicle for the toughest conditions. By 1951, with annual production nearing 20,000, it was outselling Rover saloon cars two-to-one.

It was no longer a stop-gap but a mainstay of the Rover range, as it was to be through good times and bad for 50 years. Furthermore, unlike cars that were subject to the vagaries of fashion and status, the Spartan, versatile, go-anywhere Land Rover didn't need regular titivation.

It did, however, receive constant technical development, reflecting the experience of users all over the world. Of particular significance, in view of what was to come many years later, was the seven-seater Station Wagon in 1949 but the customer response was underwhelming – partly because, in the UK, it was classified as a car, unlike the standard Land Rover which was a commercial vehicle and not subject to purchase tax.

In its first 20 years, the Land Rover became bigger, more powerful and (a little) more civilised and many more variants were made available. It became a military workhorse – for the British Army and overseas. By 1966 500,000 Land Rovers had been built in what was by then a quite separate operation from the Rover car business. Eighty per cent of all Land Rovers were exported, many of them as CKD (Completely Knocked Down) kits for assembly in faraway places.

With the original widely regarded as the world's best utility vehicle (they didn't talk about SUVs – Sport Utility Vehicles – in those days), Rover's engineering team revived earlier ideas for a Road Rover, an estate car with the comforts of a saloon but built on a Land Rover chassis.

What became the Range Rover was evolving during 1966, and took a big step forward when Rover secured the rights to manufacture a lightweight 3.5 litre V8 engine from General Motors. The specification became clear – a tall estate car with a powerful V8 engine, four-wheel drive and a Land Rover-type chassis with coil spring suspension and disc brakes on all four wheels. Charles Spencer ('Spen') King and Gordon Bashford,

Rover senior engineers, were sure that this would succeed as a dual-purpose vehicle – and satisfy an emerging US market for leisure 4X4s. Others were sceptical but the important thing was that the project gained the approval of the company's new management.

It was a time of amalgamation in the British motor industry. In 1967 Rover joined Leyland-Standard-Triumph and only a year later found itself part of the British Leyland Motor Corporation (BLMC). The formation of this massive motor group created all manner of local conflicts, particularly between the engineers at Rover and Triumph. But Land Rover was unique, a successful and profitable sideline. And Sir Donald (later Lord) Stokes, BLMC chief executive, could see the potential for the Range Rover.

So, unlike several other projects that were cast aside in the first wave of rationalisation, the Range Rover had a green light to proceed to production. But resources were scarce, so much so that King effectively designed the body himself, with the styling department only adding final cosmetic touches.

In 2001, the author was standing with Spen King when the third-generation Range Rover was unveiled and the then company chief, Wolfgang Reitzle, described it as 'a £1 billion project'. 'Did he say that it had cost a billion pounds?' asked King, incredulously. 'We produced the original Range Rover without any budget at all...'

Whilst the export-orientated Stokes had a hunch about it, there were plenty of others who saw a high-set utility vehicle with car-like attributes as a misfit. They were denied by the favourable early reviews, following the press launch in Cornwall in June 1970 that included off-roading in the Blue Hills Tin Mine. But there were some qualms: at £2,000, the Range Rover was expensive and its interior was unworthy, with expanses of

Sir William Lyons with classic Jaguars from his firm's first 25 years.

Sir William Lyons presents the E-Type, Geneva, March 1961.

Jaguar's other icon – the XJ6 saloon was introduced in 1968.

Sir John Egan took Jaguar through privatisation, later sold to Ford.

Bill Hayden, Ford manufacturing guru, headed Jaguar 1990-1992.

Sir Nick Scheele presided over Jaguar's expansion under Ford.

Jac Nasser made Jaguar a member of the Premier Automotive Group.

Jaguar takes the flag at Le Mans, 1956. C- and D-Type competition cars won the 24 Hour race five times in the 1950s.

Jaguar returned to Le Mans in the mid 1980s. The winning team of XJR9s in 1988 also took the World Sports-Prototype Championship.

Improving the breed? In 1988 the JaguarSport XJR-S, based on the then elderly XJ-S, sought to connect with its success in racing.

An unexpected brotherhood – under the skin, the 1999 Jaguar S-Type shared a majority of parts with the American Lincoln LS (left).

The original
Land Rover,
from 1948,
was intended
as a rural
workhorse.

Sir Winston
Churchill used
his Series 1
Land Rover at
Chartwell, his
country estate.

A batch of 50 pre-
production Land
Rovers were built at
the Solihull plant.

Lord Stokes, the chairman of British Leyland, could see potential in the Range Rover.

Spen King not only came up with the idea for the Range Rover but also created its distinctive style.

In 1970, the Range Rover was unique – a blend of rugged four-wheel drive vehicle and comfortable saloon.

The Discovery, introduced in 1989, bridged the gap between the definitive Land Rover and the more expensive Range Rover.

Land Rover's reputation as the most rugged and capable off-road vehicle was reinforced by using the Discovery in the Camel Trophy.

beige vinyl covering the seats and floor and ill-fitting plastic fascia mouldings.

It didn't take too long for some of these shortcomings to be addressed: smarter, brushed-nylon seat covers and proper carpet replaced the 'hose-clean' originals, and power steering was fitted. But it was a decade before four doors, automatic transmission and air conditioning were available and the car was suitable for the United States – which, for various unrelated reasons, the Range Rover would not reach until 1987.

Range Rover production, which started in November 1970, was slow at first – only 100 cars a week – and led to long waiting lists for delivery and lost export opportunities. BLMC was unwilling to make the investment at Solihull to increase production, but the 10,000 Range Rovers made in the first two years were enough to establish it as the world's best all-round 4X4 vehicle. It won a series of awards for innovation, and even found a place in an exhibition of modern design in the Louvre in Paris.

Rover and Land Rover became part of BLMC's newly created Specialist Cars Division – forming a direct relationship with Jaguar for the first time, although the engineers at both companies tried desperately to maintain their independence.

In the winter of 1973, the first oil crisis, brought about by troubles in the Middle East, cast doubts on the long-term future for big cars with large, thirsty engines. The nationalised British Leyland, formed from BLMC in 1975, was not about to spend money on Range Rover development.

In 1978, it decided to create a semi-autonomous division, Land Rover Limited, and did provide modest additional investment. Range Rover production was increased – to 450 a week – and it embarked on a programme of revisions that would bring the model's specification up to the levels of furnishing and equipment expected from a luxury saloon; in other words, it created the formula for a Range Rover that exists to this day.

With these progressive improvements, the original Range Rover stayed in production for 25 years. As it moved upmarket there was seen to be an opportunity for a cheaper vehicle, closer to the original. That emerged as the Land Rover Discovery, in 1989 – a practical, spacious vehicle with seats for seven – half-way between the utilitarian Land Rover and the latest Range Rover furnished with wood and leather.

By the time the Discovery appeared, Margaret Thatcher's Conservative government had sold still-troubled British Leyland, now renamed the Rover Group, to British Aerospace for a paltry £150 million. Ford and General Motors had both been approached and had shown interest, particularly in Land Rover, but then the prospect of selling a British asset to a foreign company became a political hot potato. Transferring ownership to British Aerospace kept it in Britain and there was much justifying talk of synergies between the automotive and defence businesses; actually, there weren't any – even with Land Rover.

In 1988, when British Aerospace took over, Land Rover accounted for 50,000 of the annual sales of Rover Group. British Aerospace presided over the development of the New Range Rover, the second generation, code-named P38A. This was an all-new vehicle that somehow managed to be less distinguished than the original (which was to continue as the Range Rover Classic until its twenty-fifth year).

Among P38A's innovations was the use of a BMW diesel engine, which seemed appropriate as, by September 1994, when the New Range Rover was launched, British Aerospace had sold the Rover Group (for £800 million and a handsome profit) to BMW. This time there were few political objections; foreign ownership was accepted as Rover's long-time associate Honda had been expected to take control when BMW's surprise bid emerged. Land Rover was the main attraction for the German company because, at that time, BMW had no SUV of its own. It later admitted that it would have paid the same amount for Land Rover alone.

At this point, Dr Wolfgang Reitzle first enters the story. Regarded as the whizz-kid of BMW, he was in charge of engineering and product development and second in command to chief executive, Bernd Pischetsrieder. Although he was enthusiastic about Land Rover – by then, approaching 100,000 sales a year – Reitzle disagreed with Pischetsrieder about acquiring the whole Rover business.

The New Range Rover didn't get off to a good start, with a series of electrical glitches compounding Land Rover's already diminished reputation for quality and reliability. Reitzle considered adapting it with the latest BMW petrol engines and mechanical improvements but decided instead to start with a clean sheet of paper to devise, as he put it, 'the best luxury 4X4 of all time'. The new vehicle, code-named L30, would share some components with BMW's 7 series saloon and was also intended to generate a high-end BMW SUV.

Within a year, Reitzle had moved into Rover as chairman and chief executive. It was a tough job and not one he wanted as it was already apparent that Rover had wider problems than BMW had realised when it rushed into purchase. In Germany, Rover began to be referred to, disparagingly, as 'The English Patient' after the then-popular Michael Ondaatjie book and film. Reitzle was frustrated by what he saw as the inefficiencies of the British system. It is fair to say that he didn't like the Rover people and they didn't much like him.

BMW's ownership was not to last. It proved unable to handle a volume brand and to reconcile British and German working practices. This was surprising as the company had the reputation of nurturing the best managers in the European motor industry. Five of its brightest stars – Pischetsrieder, Reitzle, Carl-Peter Forster, Heinrich Heitmann and Wolfgang Ziebart – departed in the wake of the Rover turmoil. Two of them would reappear in Land Rover's future.

Rover was losing £2 million a day by the time BMW left it in March 2000. BMW hoped to recoup the £1.9 billion it had to write off by selling all or part of the business. Land Rover on its own was known to be profitable but Rover Cars was hardly saleable, particularly as BMW had decided to retain the new Mini that was nearly ready for launch, and the Cowley and Hams Hall factories that were to produce it.

Ford, under Jac Nasser, was on a roll (it had made a record $7.2 billion in 1999) and pounced on Land Rover, offering £1.85 billion. After a failed bid by private equity firm Alchemy, which would have involved drastic downsizing, Rover Cars passed for a token £10 to the now-notorious Phoenix consortium of ex-Rover managers.

So Ford, which had been thwarted in its bid for Land Rover 15 years before, finally took the prize. This time, General Motors, the world's biggest motor manufacturer, did not make an offer. The reason was connected to its ownership structure. Rick Wagoner, then recently appointed GM chief executive, told the author that GM couldn't respond – or access the necessary funds – as quickly as Ford and that it was, in any case, concentrating on a major alliance with Fiat at that time.

BMW's legacy was the all-new Range Rover. Ford knew all about that as in the previous year, 1999, Nasser had set up the Premier Automotive Group (PAG) to encompass its premium brands and recruited Wolfgang Reitzle to run it. The man who had created, and lost, 'the best luxury 4X4 of all time' got it back.

Land Rover was brought into Ford's Premier Automotive Group alongside Aston Martin, Jaguar, Lincoln and Volvo. It had the closest affinity – geographically, historically, and in size and market position – to Jaguar. In July 2000, the essence of Jaguar Land Rover was born, a conjunction of British brands run by a German. This is beginning to sound familiar...

4

India's powerhouse

ALTHOUGH HIS NAME is on the door, the multinational industrial group that Ratan Tata chaired from 1991 to 2012 is not a conventional family firm. Tata Sons was founded in 1887 by Jamsetji Tata, Ratan's great-grandfather, but, today, two-thirds of the shares are owned by a number of philanthropic trusts, the biggest of which were set up by Ratan's uncle, JRD Tata. Ratan Tata, who followed JRD as chairman, has only a small personal stake, less than 1 per cent. Although undoubtedly wealthy – his PR firm emphasises that he is not a billionaire – he was always an employee, not a proprietor.

Tata is India's largest business enterprise, with interests from steel to tea bags, hotels to telecoms, chemicals to computer software, as well as trucks, buses and cars. The structure of this $100 billion business is unusual. It is a conglomerate of 96 operating companies, 31 of which are separately quoted on the Mumbai stock exchange. Many of those companies carry the Tata name, and Ratan Tata was chairman of several of them, but Tata Sons does not have a controlling interest in a single one. It describes itself as 'the promoter company', a substantial shareholder that can influence and provide guidance but not dictate policy.

The business was even more diverse before Ratan Tata took the chair. He started to restructure by reducing the number of companies under its wing and increasing Tata's shareholding in those remaining, starting new ventures in high technology, and identifying the existing operations with most growth potential. The manufacture of motor vehicles was one of those.

Tata Engineering and Locomotive Company (Telco), which became Tata Motors, had started by building trucks to serve the slowly expanding economy of newly independent India. Its first Indian-made road vehicle rolled out in 1954, a Mercedes truck licensed in an agreement with Daimler-Benz. The first Tata truck design appeared in 1969.

In the early 1990s Tata produced the Sierra, its first car-sized utility vehicle, and formed a joint venture with Daimler-Benz to manufacture Mercedes saloon cars in India. In parallel, it started development of its own car – the Indica, a small, inexpensive model for the emerging Indian car-owning class. It commissioned the body design from Italy, the engines from engineering specialists in France, and purchased nearly new production equipment from Nissan, which had just closed its Australian manufacturing operation.

Ratan Tata was personally responsible for this move into passenger cars. Speaking at the time of the Jaguar Land Rover takeover, he admitted to a passion for cars: 'Yes, I have the credit – and notoriety – of getting us into this business. Automobiles are very emotive products and the technology is very engaging.'

The Indica was presented in 1998 as the Indian national car but Tata already had its eye on export markets. It attended the international motor show in Geneva and started to solicit agents to sell its products in Europe. In retrospect, that wasn't a very good idea. In 2000, the author reported on the Tata Safari 4X4, a rough facsimile of a Land Rover Discovery with an obsolete Peugeot diesel engine, which was being offered in the UK as the cheapest full-size SUV. It was rugged and spacious but deficient in almost all other respects and could not be recommended, even at £10,000 less than the Discovery.

Indians clamoured to buy the Indica; 115,000 fully paid orders were received in its first week on sale. Many of these early customers were disappointed as India's first indigenous car had many teething troubles. After only two years, Tata had to present a modified 'V2' model to restore consumer confidence.

Then along came Rover, or rather Phoenix Venture Holdings, the company created after BMW had abandoned it. Desperate for new products but lacking the finance to create them, Phoenix agreed to become the UK distributor for the Tata Safari and Loadbeta pickup truck and to modify the Indica V2 as an entry car for the MG Rover range. It undertook to buy 100,000 over five years.

Turning the Indica into the CityRover was a rush job – and it showed. Dr V. Sumantran, the car engineering chief at what had become Tata Motors, understood the requirements (he had recently joined Tata from a senior post at General Motors in Europe) but the problem was fundamental: quality standards accepted by Indian first-time buyers were not high enough for Europe, and changing details such as springs and dampers, tyres, seat covers and floor mats was not sufficient.

Tata's first encounter with Rover was not a success and it was left with a broken contract and a lot of CityRovers waiting for shipment when Phoenix collapsed in 2005. So it is not surprising that today Tata shows little interest in using the Rover name, which it inherited when it purchased Jaguar and Land Rover from Ford (who had paid £11 million to BMW in 2006 to stop the Rover brand falling into the hands of the Chinese).

On the truck side, Tata Motors was fulfilling its international aspirations. In 2004, it acquired the commercial vehicle business of Daewoo, part of a Korean corporation that had fallen into bankruptcy. A year later, it took a 21 per cent stake in Hispano Carrocera, a Spanish bus producer (it took full control in 2009), and in 2006 formed a joint venture with Marcopolo, a leading Brazilian manufacturer of buses and coaches. It also set up a business in Thailand with Thonburi Automotive to assemble Tata pickup trucks.

By 2008, Tata Motors, already the biggest motor company in India (by revenue, when cars and commercial vehicles are put together), had become the world's fourth-largest truck maker and third-largest bus manufacturer. To symbolise its international status, the company was listed on the New York stock exchange.

Other companies in the Tata Group were spreading across the world. The biggest acquisition was British-based Corus, the Anglo-Dutch steel company, for which Tata Steel paid £6.7 billion in 2007. Tata's first major overseas investment had been a very different British institution, Tetley Tea, bought in 2000. Its Indian Hotels company grew into an international group of prestigious hotels, from the original Taj Mahal Palace in Mumbai to The Pierre on Fifth Avenue, New York.

Further emphasising the Group's diversity, Tata Consultancy Services (TCS) had gained a global reputation for software and IT systems for industry. The highest earner of all the Tata companies, TCS even provided expertise to the Ferrari Formula 1 racing team.

Ratan Tata had already formed an association with Ferrari's parent company, Fiat, through his friendship with its then-chairman, Luca di Montezemolo (also president of Ferrari), and chief executive, Sergio Marchionne. Fiat and Tata Motors embarked on several projects for mutual benefit, including sharing dealer networks in India and a joint venture to make cars and Fiat diesel engines for both brands, and Ratan Tata was invited to become a non-executive director of the Fiat Group.

In the background during this time of expansion, Ratan Tata was nurturing a long-treasured idea for a genuine Indian 'people's car'. He was concerned for the safety of Indian families – father, mother and one, often two, children – who travelled by motorcycle on the country's inadequate and congested roads. Surely the solution was a simple, back-to-basics four-wheeler, with a price not much higher than a motorbike? Ratan Tata set up a team of engineers to design such a car, which was to sell for 1 lakh (100,000 rupees, £1,250). The result was the Nano, heralded as the world's cheapest car, and launched to great enthusiasm at the New Delhi Auto Expo in January 2008. (The Nano was not to be the instant success that Tata and most onlookers had expected but that's another story.)

Coming at the time that Tata Motors was named as the favoured bidder for Jaguar and Land Rover, the Nano put even closer focus on Ratan Tata. Suddenly, everyone in the motor industry was interested in this 70-year-old man who had deter-minedly stayed out of the spotlight while building up a massive international business.

When they got to meet him, rival auto executives, journalists and analysts were surprised – and impressed. He cuts a distin-guished figure: tall, elegant, with a fine head of greying hair, and expensively dressed. He is calm, speaks softly and slowly in cultured English, and has an old world courtesy. In other words,

Ratan Tata is the antithesis of the brash, showy entrepreneurs who often represent the new wealth of India and other emerging economies.

Ratan Tata received his higher education in the United States. His BSc from Cornell University, New York, is in architecture – which helps to explain his special interest in and knowledge of car design. In 1962, after a brief spell with the Jones & Emmons architectural practice in Los Angeles, he returned to India and joined the Tata Group. He completed the Advanced Management Program at Harvard Business School in 1975.

A Parsi (a sect prominent in Indian business), he is unmarried and lives modestly in an apartment in Mumbai, surrounded, according to one biographer, by books and dogs. He owns and enjoys a small collection of classic cars, an interest fostered by childhood memories of his father's Jaguar XK120, one of the very first in India. Ratan Tata's other indulgence is to fly. A trained pilot for planes and helicopters, he likes nothing better than to take the controls of Tata's latest intercontinental jet on his way to visiting the Group's overseas operations.

Policy at Tata Sons is determined by the Global Corporate Council, a tight circle of eight of the chairman's closest associates. The Group is run by a surprisingly small staff at Bombay House, an unprepossessing 1920s building in Homi Mody Street, in the Fort district of Mumbai, which also accommodates some personnel from 25 individual Tata companies. There is nothing extravagant about Tata's headquarters: the furnishings and ambiance are more civil service than mega-business.

Tata Motors is centred in Pune, 75 miles (120 km) southeast of Mumbai, and visiting there brings another surprise. In Europe and the US, the image of industrial India is of tired, dirty and untidy premises, with employees working long hours in unhealthy conditions. But enter the gates at Tata Motors and there are constantly-swept tree-lined roads running between well-spaced buildings, peaceful garden areas, and even a nature reserve with a lake and a company guest house. It is more like a university campus than a car factory.

That says something about the company ethos, for although the vehicle assembly lines are labour-intensive and lack the latest technology, there is a clear commitment to training and employee welfare. In a classroom workshop there is a scene from another era: rows of apprentices, identically dressed in brown overalls with hard hats, standing behind benches with vices and lathes, learning metalwork and engine assembly from first principles. Tata Motors takes on 150 apprentices each year for a three-year course; most transfer from local schools. It also provides accommodation for employees recruited from outside Pune.

With annual production of 800,000 vehicles (more than 60 per cent of which are commercial vehicles), the Tata brand is not very big in global motor industry terms. It has a range of small cars, from the Nano to the Indica Vista and Indigo saloon, and the Safari and Sumo 4X4s. Its most expensive model is the Aria, which is equivalent in size and type to a European Ford S-MAX.

Tata Motors claims to be the only Indian car maker that is self-sufficient, having its own design, engineering and test facilities, including the country's only international-standard crash test facility. The Pune site, which now accommodates Land Rover Freelander and Jaguar XF assembly, already had a modern paint plant, used not only for its own products but, until recently, also for the locally assembled Mercedes-Benz C- and S-Class.

There has been much debate about whether it was an advantage or a disadvantage that Tata had no experience of premium cars before it acquired Jaguar Land Rover. On the one hand, it did not have the problem of integrating its model range with

JLR but, on the other, neither could it provide useful technology or anyone with the right credentials to run the business.

Tata would rather be seen as a strategic investor, leaving JLR as a separate entity within Tata Motors. And for that role it did have people with the right experience and authority. Ravi Kant, managing director of Tata Motors, was the person most involved with the JLR acquisition. He visited all the company's facilities and examined future programmes in fine detail, impressing those who met him with his direct and searching questions, always put with quiet Indian courtesy.

Kant, a trusted ally of Ratan Tata, joined Tata Motors in 2000. He had been in the electrical and electronics industry and transferred from Tata's Titan watch and jewellery business. Kant was appointed managing director of Tata Motors in 2005 amidst a series of overseas ventures and acquisitions in the commercial vehicle and bus sector.

A JLR executive who had regular dealings with Kant during and immediately after the takeover, describes him thus:

> He seems gentle and polite, perhaps even a bit distant and distracted, but underneath that calm exterior is a steely man. He asks the right questions and he encourages you to think big. His view is that you achieve more if you start by setting a long-term target and work back from it, rather than building up tentatively from the existing position.

If that sounds rather like his boss, Ratan Tata, it is. Both are such undemonstrative, quiet men that it is hard to detect the decisive, ruthless streak that running a major international business requires. But their results and actions speak otherwise, as a few people they appointed to JLR and subsequently discarded will confirm.

Kant is also very precise. He could allocate just one hour for an interview with the author and two colleagues in October 2008. A long and well-considered reply to the final question of the interview session wound it up, according to the digital recording, at 59 minutes and 40 seconds.

One of the reasons for that meeting was to find out how Tata's philosophy of acquisition without taking direct day-to-day management control actually works. Kant explained:

In the companies we acquire, we keep management independent – but accountable. 'Hands off' is not the same as 'left alone'; it doesn't mean we are not involved. We challenge and critique – and ask hard questions, especially where there is a need for finance.

We understand our responsibility. Once a plan is finalised we see that it is delivered. We are what we are; we don't say something and do something else.

5

Ambitions unfulfilled

J AC NASSER was known as 'Jac the Knife' but actually added
much more than he cut in his three years as Ford chief executive. Short in stature, nattily dressed and with boundless energy,
he was a man in a hurry to make his mark on the world's sec-
ond-largest car company. His biggest achievement – when Ford
profits were at an all-time high – was the expansion in premium
cars resulting from the acquisition of Volvo Cars, in 1999, and
then Land Rover in 2000.

Nasser's vision was to put all of Ford's premium marques –
Jaguar, Land Rover, Aston Martin, Lincoln and Volvo – into the
Premier Automotive Group under the direction of Dr Wolfgang
Reitzle. Getting Reitzle was quite a coup. Nasser had moved
quickly after Reitzle had been ousted from BMW in February
1999 and persuaded him that PAG represented a better opportunity than Daimler-Benz, which had also made a tempting offer.

The industry was impressed: who better to show Ford how to achieve BMW qualities than the architect of all its models since the pivotal 1986 7 series?

The Premier Automotive Group would be based in England and Reitzle, who reported directly to Nasser, insisted that its headquarters be in London, quite separate from Ford in Essex or the PAG member companies in the Midlands. He chose an elegant eighteenth-century town house in Berkeley Square, the heart of rich and fashionable Mayfair, to accommodate his 19 staff and company Aston Martin DB7 Vantage.

The individual companies would keep their own management structures and continue to be accounted separately – although Ford did not make public their results, nor those of PAG.

Nick Scheele was promoted to chairman of Ford of Europe, so Jonathan Browning was recruited from General Motors to be managing director of Jaguar, while Bob Dover, who had been in charge of Aston Martin, became Ford's first Land Rover chief executive. Dover's was a particularly appropriate appointment as, earlier in his career, he had been manufacturing director at the Solihull plant.

Reitzle was pleased to be reunited with his pet project, the L30 Range Rover. It was still a couple of years away from launch but too late in the development programme to change the BMW powertrain.* It irked Reitzle that his old company had put a high price and handling charge on the continuing supply of its engines, especially since Jaguar had a suitable V8 alternative, but he accepted that the engine swap would have to wait – until 2005, as it turned out. A similar transplant would be needed for the Freelander, the small Land Rover that had been launched in

---

* Powertrain is motor industry jargon for the combination of engine and transmission and the attendant control systems.

1997 with the Rover K-series four- and six-cylinder engines that were now in the hands of the Phoenix consortium.

The Jaguar X-Type, code-named X400, was getting ready for production and Reitzle – who sees the development of a wide range of BMW 3 series variants as one of his greatest achievements – wanted a broad spread of small Jaguars, including a new F-Type sports car which had been presented as a concept at the 2000 North American International Auto Show in Detroit. He also saw the possibility of sharing the F-Type's aluminium structure with a small Aston Martin.

Sales of the S-Type had fallen below expectations and Reitzle thought it suffered from sharing too much with the Lincoln LS and needed an upgrade that was uniquely Jaguar. (Although Nasser had planned Lincoln as an international brand, Reitzle never really got to grips with it.)

The S-Type's mid-cycle 'facelift' was brought forward and was rather more than a cosmetic makeover; the engines were revised, a German ZF six-speed automatic transmission replaced the original's slow-witted American five-speed, and a powerful R model was introduced to rival the BMW M5 as the world's fastest sports saloon.

Meanwhile, plans laid earlier to replace the Jaguar XJ with a car made largely in aluminium were progressing and a new kind of production line was being devised to rivet and glue, rather than weld, its body panels. Not surprisingly, Reitzle championed this new technology, which he believed would give Jaguar the special character that a premium brand needs.

On the industrial side, things were looking up. In 2000, the respected research firm J.D. Power gave Jaguar's Browns Lane factory first place in its European Plant Awards; the rebuilding and reorganisation that followed Bill Hayden's 'Gorky' outburst a decade before had paid off. A Jaguar team led by David Hudson had transformed the Halewood assembly plant to start X-Type production. When it was making Ford Escorts, Halewood had a terrible reputation for quality, productivity and labour relations but Jaguar raised standards to such an extent that it came to be rated among the best of Ford's plants worldwide. Jaguar's new association with Land Rover was to show itself for the first time when Freelander production was transferred there from Solihull.

Ford had inherited a state-of-the-art technical centre at Gaydon, Warwickshire as part of the Land Rover deal with BMW. Although it intended to maintain Jaguar's Whitley engineering facility, the Gaydon site, which includes a test track, benefited both marques – and Aston Martin, which was to build a new factory there.

PAG was starting to gain momentum, particularly with the integration of its British brands. But back in Dearborn, storm clouds were gathering over Ford World Headquarters. After forming PAG, Jac Nasser had gone on a spending spree, buying a number of companies that were peripheral to the car business with the intention of turning Ford into a 'full consumer service company'. He then faced a crisis created by accidents blamed on inadequate Firestone tyres fitted to Ford Explorers in the US.

Ford's share price tumbled, it suffered consecutive quarterly losses for the first time in ten years, and its cash pile had disappeared. The Ford board of directors, primarily representing the Ford family, decided Nasser had to go. He was fired on 30 October 2001 by chairman Bill Ford, who reluctantly took over as chief executive.

As one of his closest lieutenants, Reitzle was discomfited by Nasser's departure – and the cost-cutting that he knew would follow. Over two-and-a-half years, he had made PAG his own fiefdom – the industry joked that it was to be renamed RAG, for Reitzle Automotive Group.

He had turned the idea of platform-sharing with other Ford companies on its head and wanted PAG to take responsibility for creating its own unique products. Reitzle explained his philosophy in several interviews with the author in 2000 and 2001:

> Focusing on cost alone will always dilute a premium brand. There is nothing wrong with centrally developing core components that do not determine the brand character but for those that do, PAG should define the top specification. Then our basic architecture can be used throughout Ford, upgrading its technology as well as achieving economies of scale. I call this the highest common denominator.
>
> Today (in November 2001) we ask for help when we need it and for parts and components we would like to have but we are no longer told what we have to take. My ambition is that whenever we have a new product, we start from scratch, with no compromises.

Less than a month after Nasser had gone, Reitzle stood at the microphone in the London Design Museum to introduce a product that he had started from scratch, with no compromises, some years before – the third-generation Range Rover.

The audience was stunned when he declared that the L30, which became Ford project L322, had cost £1 billion to develop – the same as the contemporary BMW 7 series but considerably more than most new high-volume cars at that time. And he promised that the implementation of BMW processes on the new production line at Solihull would ensure that its quality matched the 7 series and Mercedes S-Class, the luxury cars which he regarded as the Range Rover's real competitors.

It was BMW, rather than Ford, which had carried most of that £1 billion. Reitzle knew that PAG was unlikely ever to have such a large development budget for a single model. But the same evening in London he publicly floated the idea of a range of Range Rovers: now that the flagship was approaching Bentley in luxury and price, he could see a place for a smaller, sportier and less expensive Range Rover based on the Land Rover Discovery.

That vehicle, the Range Rover Sport, was to emerge in 2005 and become Land Rover's best-selling – and most profitable – model. By then, the 'full-size' Range Rover had met Reitzle's original objective. It was proclaimed king of the 4X4s in all the major markets, and in Britain it outsold all the top executive saloons: the BMW 7 series, Mercedes S-Class, Audi A8 – and the Jaguar XJ.

Land Rover and Jaguar moved ever closer when, early in 2002, Bob Dover was given overall charge of both brands plus Aston Martin and set up a central staff of 100 people at Gaydon to serve PAG's 'British motor corporation'. Its production was at an all-time high – the combined volume of Land Rover and Jaguar would top 300,000 in 2002 – but across the Atlantic at Ford head-quarters, the financial situation was reaching crisis point.

On a snowy day in January 2002, as the North American International Auto Show was opening in nearby Detroit, Ford gathered together business journalists and industry analysts at the conference centre next to the Henry Ford Museum in Dearborn. Bill Ford and his chosen second in command, Nick Scheele, outlined a 'revitalisation programme' which involved cutting costs in all aspects of its business.

The headlines were that five factories would be closed and 35,000 jobs lost, but Scheele emphasised: 'We have cut costs everywhere, from cancelling coffee at meetings to disposing of several corporate aircraft.' That was to have some resonance six years later when chief executives of Detroit's 'Big Three' (Ford, GM and Chrysler) were criticised for flying in company jets to Washington, when they went for crisis talks with the US government.

Significantly, at the Dearborn meeting, Scheele also said that the cuts would not apply to the Premier Automotive Group: 'It is a fundamental part of our strategy going forward. We expect PAG to contribute one-third of Ford's global profits by 2005.'

Despite that reassurance, it soon became clear that Reitzle's grand plan could not be sustained in these difficult times for the mother ship. Reitzle resigned, ostensibly because he now had to report to president Scheele rather than chairman Bill Ford, but he could see the writing on the wall.

There is no doubt that Reitzle's drive and dedication, and his attention to design and engineering detail, were beneficial to Jaguar and Land Rover. Directly or indirectly, he gave both marques the best range of vehicles they had ever had and he formed a much better relationship with them than he had at Rover. Indeed, 'the Doctor' still appears at Gaydon and Whitley from time to time as an informal advisor to Tata.

At Ford, though, there were people who were pleased to see the back of Reitzle. Notable among them was his rival, David Thursfield, who had followed Scheele as chairman of Ford of Europe. Reiztle and Thursfield had a celebrated battle of egos about who should take prominence at an event at the Bridgend engine plant which made (and still makes) the Jaguar V8 engine alongside a much higher volume of four-cylinder engines for Ford cars. Thursfield was himself to leave the company in May 2004.

It was no surprise that soon after Reitzle left PAG, the F-Type was cancelled (the message was that the money would be put into diesel engines instead), the prestigious office in Berkeley Square was closed and the Jaguar Formula 1 racing team was curtailed.

Jaguar's venture into Grand Prix racing had been Nasser's idea – Ford had taken over Jackie Stewart's team and he thought that a prestigious brand that made sports cars was more appropriate for Formula 1 than blue-collar Ford. He hoped to 'win on Sunday and sell on Monday' but the team, which cost a fortune and had a succession of high-profile racing managers – including three-times World Champion Niki Lauda – didn't achieve a single victory in five years and 85 races. To add to the humiliation, its Milton Keynes premises and many of the staff were taken on by Red Bull Racing – which was to win the World Championship three years in a row from 2010.

The new president of PAG, Mark Fields, had made his name as president of Mazda, the Japanese car maker which Ford controlled. A 41-year-old American, he was known for his conciliatory people skills and business school protocol; quite a contrast to Reitzle, the curt German technocrat who always liked to be seen to be in charge.

The polished silver, all-aluminium, XJ shone brightly on the Jaguar stand at the Paris Motor Show in September 2002. This car, code-named X350, five years in preparation and utilising construction principles first developed at Ford in America, was heralded as the boldest move since Ford bought the company. It was a significant engineering achievement: 200 kg lighter than its predecessor, it offered better performance *and* improved fuel economy. But, despite the eloquent claims of design director Ian Callum – who had joined Jaguar in 1999 after designing the glorious Aston Martin DB7 – the XJ's appearance had hardly changed. That was to prove a serious error.

Bob Dover, soon to be promoted to chairman and chief executive of Jaguar and Land Rover, understood what was at stake. 'People don't buy technology, they buy benefits,' he said at the XJ's press preview at Goodwood House in Sussex. But on the conservative styling, he was adamant: 'Our customers said: don't change it, just make it better.'

The folklore is that Jaguar was forbidden from making a radical change to its flagship model by the Ford family and the American top management – many of whom enjoyed Jaguars as their personal cars. Also, that market research, which Ford took very seriously, consistently found that Jaguar buyers favoured retaining the shape and style begun with William Lyons' 1968 XJ6.

Some of those closely involved at the time say that, actually, the main proponents of the old style were in Jaguar management in Coventry, that there was little pressure from Dearborn, and the market intelligence came more from the US dealers than their customers.

Whatever the reason, the new-old XJ was not to be the success that Jaguar expected. Perhaps a lesson should have been learned from Audi, which had earlier produced an aluminium A8 and quickly discovered that the majority of buyers either didn't know or didn't care what it was made from. That turned out also to be true for Jaguar. Its loyal customers finally tired of the 35-year-old XJ look and went for more obviously modern alternatives available from rival premium brands.

In any case, the premium market in Europe was changing. Diesel engines were becoming more popular – apart from being more economical, in some countries the fuel was cheaper and they brought tax advantages. About 50 per cent of the BMWs sold in Europe were diesel-powered. Jaguar, and Ford, should have anticipated this demand, but didn't, and so the X-Type was launched in 2001 with petrol engines only and would not offer a diesel until September 2003. The S-Type diesel was introduced the following year and its engine finally reached the XJ a year after that.

The traditional XJ styling notwithstanding, 2003 was when Jaguar set a new pattern for the future. With authorities and consumers placing an increasing emphasis on fuel economy, lightweight aluminium was the way to go, even if it was more expensive than steel; four different JLR model series would use this construction by 2013. The diesel engine, once unthinkable in a Jaguar, gave the X-Type a new lease of life and this model destroyed two more shibboleths by having a four-cylinder engine and front-wheel drive.

It used to be that a six-, eight- or 12-cylinder engine and rear-wheel drive were essential elements of any Jaguar. That is why the original X-Types, based on a front-wheel drive Ford Mondeo platform, had V6 engines and four-wheel drive. By 2013, both Jaguar saloons (XF and XJ) would offer four-cylinder versions and four-wheel drive – although the latter is for different reasons to the X-Type. Front-wheel drive alone has not been used since the demise of the X-Type in 2009 but, inevitably, will reappear if and when Jaguar introduces a much smaller car.

In 2004, it was clear that even with a four-car range (XJ, S-Type, X-Type and XK) Jaguar sales were not going to get anywhere near Ford's long-held ambitions. Fields, with a couple of years in charge of PAG and now having the greater responsibility of Ford of Europe, concluded that Jaguar, which was losing money as an individual entity, could not justify three factories. Among volume car makers at that time, 300,000 was the optimum annual production for one plant. Jaguar was making 120,000 at three. One had to be closed – and it would be Browns Lane, Coventry.

The task of shutting down Jaguar's ancestral home was passed to Joe Greenwell, recently appointed chairman and chief executive of Jaguar and Land Rover. He admitted that it was a tough job because he had an emotional attachment to Browns Lane, having worked there for most of his career and been public relations chief through the Scheele era. Browns Lane ceased production in July 2005 and assembly of the XJ and XK was transferred to Castle Bromwich.

Jaguar enthusiasts were outraged but the business logic was undeniable. In September 2005, as he left Europe to take charge of all Ford's American operations, Fields reflected on the diminished prospects for Jaguar – which by then was making fewer than 90,000 cars a year. 'Don't look at Jaguar as a smaller version of Ford,' he counselled, 'It's more like a big Aston Martin.'

Fields handed over Ford of Europe and PAG to Lewis Booth, a Brit who had followed him as president of Mazda. By the time of Fields' departure, PAG was becoming irrelevant. Volvo was now more closely allied to Ford's volume brands, as it began to use component sets from the Ford Global Shared Technology programme. Lincoln had been returned to American administration and Aston Martin, run by Ulrich Bez, was allowed virtual autonomy with its own, versatile VH (Vertical, Horizontal) aluminium platform system.

Jaguar and Land Rover remained united, offering very different vehicles in the same market sector. Jaguar's V8 engine was eminently suitable for the Range Rover (and finally found its way there in 2005) and the new Ford-produced diesel engines could be used by both marques, along with developments in control systems and electronics.

In August 2006 there was the first indication that Jaguar might be for sale. It became known that Ford had commissioned Kenneth Leet, a mergers and acquisitions specialist from Goldman Sachs, to 'explore strategic alternatives' for its car-making operations. 'The Way Forward', the follow-up to Ford's revitalisation plan, wasn't working – Ford was to lose $5.8 billion in the third quarter of 2006 – and chief financial officer

Don Leclair needed to present to the board various options for keeping the company afloat.

It had already been decided to sell Aston Martin; this prestige marque was doing well, with production at 7,000 cars a year, and was expected to raise up to $1 billion. Analysts surmised that Jaguar, which was haemorrhaging money (unofficial estimates put its annual losses at more than $700 million), would not be saleable on its own and the offer would have to be made more attractive by adding in Land Rover, which generated as much as $1 billion annual profit.

A month later, Alan Mulally arrived at Ford World Headquarters from Boeing, where he had achieved an impressive turnround in its commercial aircraft division. He had been wooed by Bill Ford and came to the company as chief executive, with carte blanche to restore it to health and profitability.

Among Mulally's first thoughts was a reorganisation concentrating on just one brand. He assessed that management was spread too thinly; it wasn't able to cope adequately with the main Ford brand and so should not be diverted by low-volume, high-cost subsidiaries. It was then, at the moment when the 'One Ford' strategy formed in his mind, that Ford effectively said goodbye to Jaguar and Land Rover.

6

Premium brands for sale

O N 12 MARCH 2007, at a hastily convened press conference in the airy lobby of Aston Martin's palatial new headquarters at Gaydon, Lewis Booth announced that Ford had concluded negotiations to sell Aston Martin.

There had been weeks of speculation about which of the many companies, large and small, famous and obscure, that had shown interest would secure the boutique car brand that Ford had acquired 20 years before. Booth, as chairman of Ford of Europe and the Premier Automotive Group, introduced the successful bidder as a consortium funded by Adeem and Investment Dar, investment companies from Kuwait. It was to pay $925 million for Aston Martin.

Booth said that it was a 'bittersweet day' for Ford. He had been assured by the new owners that Aston production would be maintained and expanded and that existing management under

Ulrich Bez would remain in place. For its part, Ford agreed to continue to supply parts and services. Oh, and he added as a postscript, Jaguar and Land Rover, who had their administration buildings on the same Gaydon site, were not for sale.

It was true: Jaguar and Land Rover were not for sale – then. But Booth was acutely aware of Alan Mulally's One Ford plan and Ford's deteriorating financial position. Even before Mulally had joined, finance director, Don Leclair, warned that credit lines were tightening and had made the first moves to access the cash that Ford would need to survive a painful period of restructuring. Mulally went to Wall Street with a plan to borrow $23.6 billion by mortgaging the company's assets: factories, offices, equipment, intellectual property – everything. Analysts noted that, while even the famous Ford blue oval logo was in hock, Jaguar and Land Rover properties were not. So their disposal would surely come.

The announcement was three months later. Investment banks Goldman Sachs and Morgan Stanley had been instructed to make a valuation of the Jaguar and Land Rover business, to sound out potential buyers, and ultimately to help Ford to achieve a successful sale. The banks were to filter serious expressions of interest from the dozens of unsuitable applicants – ambitious but clearly underfunded companies and individuals, would-be car makers with no concept of the business, and the inevitable chancers and time-wasters.

The two brands were to be sold together. This was not only because profitable Land Rover could offset loss-making Jaguar but also because their technical and manufacturing integration made it impractical to separate them. Furthermore, Ford wanted to sell 100 per cent; Mulally was serious about needing management to concentrate on the Blue Oval, with no diversions.

Once again, the job of chief negotiator fell to Lewis Booth. He confessed to having mixed emotions selling companies that he had led and worked with over many years. As well as dismantling PAG (Volvo was to be sold to the Chinese company Geely 18 months after the JLR disposal), Booth saw Ford cash in most of its shareholding in Mazda, where he had been president.

Although he had worked for Ford all around the world, Booth, a qualified engineer and accountant, started in the motor industry as a graduate trainee at British Leyland in Longbridge, Birmingham. He now felt an obligation to safeguard the last major car manufacturer in the British Midlands; he was a Brit, selling a British business run by long-standing colleagues, and he had established relationships with all the interested parties, from the UK government and the European Union to the trade unions. Mulally understood that Ford's reputation, as market leader in the UK, was at stake and left Booth to conduct the sale in conjunction with finance chief, Leclair.

The target price was around $3 billion but Booth and Mulally agreed that money alone would not determine the successful bidder. As far as possible, they wanted the business to survive intact without loss of jobs and with security for the intellectual property that would have to be transferred.

An existing car manufacturer seemed to be the best possibility for such an outcome. But the motor industry had just come through a round of consolidation, General Motors was feeling the same stresses as Ford, and the main European players were not in a buying mood. Asked by journalists at the time, Fiat, Peugeot and Renault all said they were not interested. There were reports of talks with Hyundai of Korea and fledgling Chinese car makers but evidently they came to nothing.

Unexpectedly, the two motor companies that did enter the bidding were from India. Tata Motors had been encouraged by

Lord Bhattacharyya, chairman of the Warwick Manufacturing Group at Warwick University, a leading light in the regional development organisation Advantage West Midlands, and a personal friend of Ratan Tata. Tata's rival, Mahindra & Mahindra, was well known to Ford as they once had a joint venture in India.

The two Indian manufacturers found themselves on the narrowed-down prospect list with a number of private equity firms. Many of the recent moves in the auto world had involved this kind of investment; in America, Cerberus Capital Management had just paid $7.4 billion to buy Chrysler out of its disastrous merger with Daimler.

Four of the private equity companies that went forward were advised by a former senior executive from Ford or JLR: Jac Nasser was a partner in One Equity Partners; Nick Scheele joined up with Ripplewood Holdings; Bob Dover was linked to TPG Capital; and Cerberus employed David Thursfield. When deputations from these firms were given fact-finding tours at Gaydon, some of JLR's management found it daunting to make presentations to their former bosses who already knew the secrets of the business.

Booth was in a difficult situation. His job was to get the best deal for Ford but he had to keep JLR going at an undiminished rate during the sale process; if there was to be continuity between the old and new owners, business reviews, investment, and work on new models had to be maintained until the handover. At the same time, Ford's advisors – the investment banks, lawyers and accountants – demanded a large amount of time and information to compile detailed marketing and diligence materials for distribution to the serious prospects. Accountants KPMG put a team into a rented office in Solihull, nearby to Gaydon, for easy access. Each department had to be reviewed to decide which functions could be transferred to a stand-alone company and which would remain with Ford and, of the latter, which could have long-term supply agreements with the buyer.

All this demanded loyalty and commitment from people who faced an uncertain future. Booth paid tribute to Geoff Polites, chief executive of Jaguar and Land Rover since 2005, and the senior management, for their leadership during this period and for staying focused when the company was under constant review. He said, with some pride: 'They didn't miss a beat.'

Actually, they did much more, vigorously promoting Jaguar and Land Rover with a combination of hard facts and honest enthusiasm. Outside observers had described Jaguar as a 'basket case' and joked that, since most bidders were primarily interested in the potential for Land Rover, the proposition was 'buy one and get one free'.

In August, JLR executive director Mike Wright – who had already served four owners and been a managing director of Land Rover UK and Jaguar, separately and together, at different times – and a team of senior colleagues, organised two-day seminars for each of seven companies on the first shortlist.

On the first day, each group (typically of 30 or more people) had a factory visit, a presentation on current and future products, and an opportunity to experience them driven flat out on the Gaydon test track by Mike Cross, JLR's famed car-handling expert (his title was, and is, head of vehicle integrity). The presentation by JLR senior management was on the second day, with the financials left until last.

Showing the hardware before the numbers was clever. The immediate feedback was that the prospective bidders found a business far more confident than they had expected, with an impressive product plan and what seemed like a realistic prospect of a profitable future.

When it came to judging the first bids, Ford and its advisors had to take a view on whether the potential owners would be able to deliver their visions for the two brands. Booth worried that, by their nature, private equity firms would need to sell all or part of the company at some stage.

One Equity, well funded and a division of J.P. Morgan investment bank, could be an exception, simply because of Nasser's enthusiasm for the premium car business. As Nasser had been removed as chief executive only six years before, Ford might have been cautious about his bid but it had determined not to be influenced by previous animosities. Indeed, when the author met Nasser during the selection process, he was optimistic about One Equity's chances.

As the owner of demerged Chrysler, Cerberus could present itself as a car maker as well as a private equity finance company. The bid by Mahindra & Mahindra was also linked to private equity.

It came down to a final shortlist of three: One Equity, Tata Motors and Cerberus. None of the unsuccessful bidders talked about how and why they fell by the wayside – and Ford had no need to explain – but it seems that Mahindra & Mahindra was losing interest. Mahindra & Mahindra, a diverse business in which the manufacture of tractors and light trucks played the major part, had a plan for Land Rover to complement its own products but was uncertain about Jaguar.

The finalists in this contest to secure Ford's crown jewels were given access to the 'big data room' where, for a limited period, all the books, including sensitive commercial contracts, were open and their teams of advisors could assess the financial details of the business under offer.

At the same time, each conducted an exhausting series of meetings with Ford, JLR management, government departments and representatives of the workforce. These took place mostly on neutral ground, in the London offices of advisors to the various parties; a favoured location was the office of Ford lawyers Hogan & Hartson, overlooking the steps of St Paul's Cathedral.

Renewing old acquaintances, Nasser worked hard to get the unions to approve his bid. Tata was able to get the government's attention by pointing to its track record with Corus steel, which it had acquired in the past year. Cerberus talked of synergies with the Chrysler product line, which included Jeep, Land Rover's only direct rival.

On 3 January 2008, Ford announced that Tata was its preferred bidder. Again, no reason was given but it can be assumed that Tata matched the best financial bid, while promising the least disruption and the strongest commitment to future growth for both marques. Ratan Tata's personal enthusiasm for the whole business may also have helped and that Tata were a trade buyer, rather than a private equity company, meant that they saw JLR as a long-term acquisition. Reflecting on the decision later, Booth said: 'Towards the end it was a matter of chemistry. Tata saw the future for the business broadly as we did. We seemed to be closely aligned.'

There was a lot to be sorted out. Tata Motors was a very different business to Jaguar and Land Rover. There was very little opportunity for component sharing between the owner and its purchase, which meant that long-term agreements would have to be made about intellectual property and the supply of power-trains and many other parts and services.

Ford was prepared for an 18-month transition period for most management services but wanted its finance company, Ford Motor Credit, disentangled from JLR within nine months.

A team from Tata moved into Gaydon for a more thorough investigation, preparatory to a final bid. Meanwhile, Mike

Wright was setting up new financial services arrangements and working out how to separate JLR from 25 national sales companies owned by Ford. In most cases that meant starting from scratch, as Tata Motors was not present in many of the same countries. Jaguar and Land Rover did not even have a sales company in India.

On 26 March 2008, Ford and Tata were able to announce an agreement. Tata Motors would purchase 100 per cent of Jaguar and Land Rover for $2.3 billion, while Ford would contribute $600 million to top up the pension fund for the transferred employees.

So the deal was done. Tata pledged to nurture the brands, accepted the JLR forward product plan and promised expansion in production, research and geographic spread. Ford received some much-needed cash and no longer had to devote management time and effort to a peripheral overseas subsidiary. No matter that it had invested some $10 billion in the two brands over the years, with very little return. That was the past – and, in this case, the past really was another country.

Booth was satisfied with the outcome. Discussing it with the author in November 2012, he said: 'It was hard for me emotionally but I genuinely believe it was the right thing for Jaguar Land Rover. I feel very good about the way that Ford handled the company until the day we sold it and the way Tata has treated it since.'

Shortly after the sale, Booth moved to Ford World Headquarters in Dearborn to replace Leclair as chief financial officer and become Mulally's right-hand man. This new job looked like a poisoned chalice; it was an awful time to take charge of Ford's finances and the results were getting worse every quarter. But by the summer of 2009 the US car market was showing the first signs of recovery and Mulally's restructuring had begun to take effect. In America, Ford was to go on to near-record profits (although Ford of Europe was still struggling), so when Booth retired from Ford in April 2012, it was with honour.

Appropriately, Booth's work was also acknowledged in his home country as he was appointed Commander of the British Empire (CBE) in the Queen's Birthday Honours list for 2012. The citation reads: 'For services to the UK automotive and manufacturing industries.' One of those services was to deliver Jaguar Land Rover into a safe pair of hands.

7

Tata's inheritance

OPINIONS WERE DIVIDED on whether the $2.3 billion that Tata paid Ford was too high a price for Jaguar Land Rover. Those who saw no future for Jaguar thought it was a high value for Land Rover alone. Others were sceptical about Tata's chances of success. If a huge motor manufacturer like Ford didn't think JLR was worth keeping, how would an Indian company with no experience in premium cars make it work?

More cynical observers, including some UK politicians, argued that Tata had simply paid a lot of money for two well-known brands and that, before long, JLR's equipment and expertise would be shipped off to India, leaving the West Midlands as an automotive wasteland. They reminded of the promises made by the Chinese manufacturer Nanjing Automotive when it acquired the remains of MG Rover and said it would revive mass-production at Longbridge.

People close to Ford said that $2.3 billion was a bargain price: half, perhaps a third, of what JLR was really worth. The business was on course to make a good profit from a series of new products that were ready for launch – and were handed over as part of the sale. If Ford had hung on, they said, JLR would have sold for much more.

For Alan Mulally, with Ford facing continuing losses and declining sales, hanging on wasn't an option. Lewis Booth and Don Leclair had to sell JLR in a buyers' market and it is hard to lift the price if there is not much competition.

Also, Ford had agreed that, if it could, it would sell JLR to an organisation that intended to preserve all the main elements of the business. Tata was the highest bidder with what Ford assessed as a deliverable long-term programme.

If there were some doubts in the UK, the reaction in Indian financial circles was even less favourable. Investors in Tata Motors reacted to the news of the JLR acquisition by selling stock. In the weeks that followed, the share price dropped 77 per cent from its previous high. A rights issue intended to fund the purchase was a damp squib. Instead, Tata was forced to arrange $3 billion bridging finance piecemeal from 21 different lenders.

In India, the investment bank Morgan Stanley reported that acquiring JLR appeared to be a negative move for Tata Motors. It increased earnings volatility, because of the difficult economic conditions in JLR's key markets, and promised to involve large additional capital expenditure on new models. This cautious pessimism was understandable at that time but even the most visionary of investors who held on to Tata Motors stock would not have expected the huge rise in the company's value within four years – generated by JLR's success.

Tata inherited a lot of property at the time of the takeover. There were three manufacturing plants – Castle Bromwich,

Halewood and Solihull – and two extensive and well-equipped technical centres at Gaydon and Whitley, which could also accommodate management and administration. The deal included royalty-free licences for a raft of intellectual property rights and a worldwide network of national sales companies. When sold, JLR had 16,000 staff, including 3,500 employed in engineering, product development and research.

The sales figures for 2007 that became available as Tata was going through due diligence indicated a record year for Land Rover and the second-highest volume for Jaguar and Land Rover combined: 286,880.

Land Rover's total of 226,395 was 18 per cent up on the previous year (which was itself a record) and since 89,000 of those sales were Range Rover and Range Rover Sport – known to be among the most profitable vehicles in the whole Ford empire – the estimate of the brand's earnings of more than $1 billion seemed realistic.

By contrast, Jaguar's numbers told a story of continuing decline. The 60,485 sales total for 2007 was 24 per cent down year-on-year and less than half that of its best annual performance in 2002. More worryingly, it was well below the 80,000 that Ford used to say was the break-even point for Jaguar alone.

Closer integration with Land Rover had lowered that break-even figure, as did a drive to build up transaction prices (the amount the customer actually pays, including extras, and after discounts and incentives). Jaguar had already had some success in achieving a richer mix of sales; at the time of the XF launch, early in 2008, managing director Mike O'Driscoll said that it could make money on 65,000 cars a year.

However, it was clear to Tata, as it had been to Ford, that Jaguar needed more work. Ford had already taken the big decision, rejecting the old style and giving the go-ahead for the very different XF and the new XJ. Tata could benefit immediately, as the XF went on sale just as it was taking over: a bright new model promising a new start.

But it was also clear that there was a fundamental flaw in the whole Jaguar model strategy. Its German competitors used their big and expensive limousines and sports cars to set their image but made their money from the smaller and cheaper models that sold in much higher numbers.

Jaguar's smallest car, the X-Type, was withering on the vine: sales had dwindled from a peak of 73,000 to 23,000. Even the most optimistic projections put sales of the new XF and forthcoming XJ at about the same level as the best years for their predecessors (20,000–30,000 each). The XK sports coupe and convertible, launched as new models in 2006, had reached the same volume (12,000) as the previous model but there was still a price chasm beneath them, which the Porsche Boxster, Mercedes SLK and BMW Z4 had eagerly filled.

It was no surprise that Tata found Land Rover in good shape in its sixtieth year. All of its models apart from the evergreen Defender had been renewed or substantially revised in the previous three years. The Discovery, which had largely taken the Defender's role as the farmer's friend, had a new style as the Discovery 3; some said that its clean, unfussy lines were 'brutalist', but it had won awards for industrial design. The smallest Land Rover, the Freelander, had finally discarded its Rover and BMW connections to share components with the Ford S-MAX, Galaxy and Volvo S80, and its sales had gone up to 66,500, not far off the best years for the original, which had faced far fewer competitors. But the real star was the Range Rover Sport.

It was Wolfgang Reitzle's idea to produce a Range Rover at a lower price than the flagship model by using the chassis structure from the Land Rover Discovery. As it was lower and lighter

– and a touch smaller – than the genuine article, the Sport could at least go some way to living up to its name. But it was the unmistakable styling and presentation that sold it – an invitation to join the Range Rover club with a lower entry fee. The Sport sold for 25 per cent less than the Range Rover but the production cost was lower still, so it is no wonder that it was JLR's most profitable product. And in 2006, its second year, it was also Land Rover's highest seller.

The Range Rover Sport increased sales further, to 58,800 in 2007, more than 10,000 ahead of the mechanically similar Land Rover Discovery, which was more versatile and spacious but didn't have the same luxurious features – or the same caché. The Sport taught JLR a lot about brand values and premium marketing, lessons it would put to wider use and good effect.

Future direction at the other end of its product range – where Land Rover started – was less certain. The utilitarian Defender still sold around 25,000 a year but no longer had much in common with the other models. Increasingly, it was bought for leisure use rather than the agricultural, public service and military functions for which it was designed. JLR recognised the Defender as the bedrock of Land Rover but couldn't decide how to replace it.

Tata might have been expected to intervene here as the Defender was the one JLR vehicle that cut across Tata's own product range. Wouldn't it be logical for the next Defender and a Tata 4X4 to share the same structure and to be made more cheaply in India? Tata Motors managing director, Ravi Kant, was quick to put down that idea. He reminded everyone that taking JLR technology to India was not part of the plan and anyway, he said, 'I don't believe you can transpose vehicle DNA in that way.'

The biggest cloud on Land Rover's horizon was made of carbon dioxide. Land Rover had survived periodic attacks from environmentalists who labelled its cars socially irresponsible 'gas guzzlers' – one campaign asked the question 'What would Jesus drive?' and got some amusing responses – but now legislation and consumer pressure were demanding better fuel efficiency and lower carbon dioxide emissions.

Downsizing was the new industry buzz-word. Lighter vehicles could have smaller engines and better fuel economy while maintaining the performance of heavy ones. Small cars could provide the attributes, fittings and equipment of larger models. The challenge was, in mature markets at least, to break the connection between size and status.

Land Rover had started work on an aluminium Range Rover but also realised that it would need to offer more choices in and below the Freelander class. The LRX, which made its debut at the 2008 Detroit Auto Show a few days after Tata had been confirmed as the preferred bidder for JLR, demonstrated an exciting way of extending the small car range. Unlike the Jaguar C-XF presented a year earlier, LRX was a pure concept car (design director Gerry McGovern described it as 'a white space car'), rather than a preview of a production model.

Recognising that small SUVs with car-like characteristics were the growth market, Ford had included such a vehicle in JLR's future product plan. The snazzy coupe-style LRX – very different from existing small SUVs and crossovers – looked promising but some thought that it might be too extreme for the market. It hadn't been approved for production when the company was sold, although JLR's American product development director, Al Kammerer, confided to the author that it was '75 per cent ready'. It would be down to Tata to decide whether to go ahead.

After a thorough review of the business and its present and future products, Tata was pleased with its purchase. The due diligence had brought no nasty surprises. Seeing how anxious

Ford had been to sell it, some commentators painted a bleak prospect for JLR but actually Ford's business plan set out a bright and profitable future. It needed investment and that Tata was prepared to make.

At a simple ceremony at Gaydon to mark the official handover on completion of the acquisition on 2 June 2008, Ratan Tata summed up Tata's initial assessment of JLR: 'We recognise the significant improvement in performance of the two brands and look forward to this trend continuing in the coming years.'

Neither he, nor anyone else present that day, anticipated the economic hurricane that was on its way and how quickly JLR's promising performance would go into reverse.

8

Business as usual

TATA HAD PLENTY OF EXPERIENCE of managing established brands and knew that there is a delicate balance between leaving well alone and exerting influence to try to accelerate sales and profit. Discussing Jaguar Land Rover at the Bangkok Motor Show just days after the takeover was confirmed, Ravi Kant told reporters: 'We have seen the five-year business plan prepared by the Jaguar Land Rover management and we have bought into that fully.'

That business plan had been developed by the team led by Geoff Polites, who had been appointed chief executive of Jaguar and Land Rover in October 2005, arriving from Ford Australia by way of Ford of Europe. Polites was well liked within the company as a no-nonsense Australian who had worked in the retail car trade and had a good grasp of consumer needs and tastes. He had aligned with those in the company who wanted to drop the Jaguar 'country house' style once and for all, and drove through the radical (for Jaguar) XF and XJ designs as well as the Land Rover LRX concept.

Polites was diagnosed with terminal cancer soon after he moved to the UK. He worked tirelessly while undergoing long courses of medical treatment but succumbed to the disease in April 2008. Rumour had it that Tata had already decided to appoint a new chief executive. On 6 January, while due diligence was in progress, *The Sunday Times* reported that Tata intended to install an unnamed senior Ford executive into the top job at JLR.

Tata's choice was David Smith, director of finance and business strategy at Ford of Europe. Lewis Booth had agreed that Smith, who had previously worked at PAG in Gaydon, should transfer to the new company as finance director and chief executive-in-waiting. Smith took over as acting chief executive when Polites died and would be confirmed in the job at the formal handover to Tata on 2 June.

Otherwise, there was little change to the JLR management structure. Mike O'Driscoll continued as managing director of Jaguar and Phil Popham held the equivalent job at Land Rover. Both Brits, O'Driscoll had transferred the previous year from heading Jaguar Land Rover North America, while Popham had joined Land Rover as a graduate trainee in 1988 and worked his way up to the top of the brand in 2006.

Smith was an unlikely captain of industry. He was brought up in Solihull, not far from the Land Rover factory in Lode Lane, and studied economics at Cambridge, but instead of joining his fellow graduates in the City, decided on a career in the motor industry. Although he had progressed through the rough-and-tumble of Ford, he was almost shy in public, with the studious bearing of an academic rather than a thrusting businessman.

Tata was true to its principles: appoint a manager and allow him to get on with the job with minimum interference. Initially, JLR was directed by a three-man board: Ratan Tata, Kant and Smith. In an interview with the author in July 2009, Smith revelled in his freedom of action: 'The governance is very simple. I am allowed to get on and run the business and we go through the plans once or twice a month. For my team, it is really empowering – and quite different for someone who was 25 years with Ford.'

There was logic in appointing a finance man to run a business that had been separated from an all-embracing multinational corporation. For the first time, Jaguar Land Rover had to generate its own management accounts, control its own balance sheet and watch its own cashflow. Smith personally tutored JLR's senior executives in 20 half-day sessions on cashflow management.

Smith had to separate financial services, employee contracts and pensions, and myriad other elements from the Ford Motor Company and set up new disciplines for the new company. Tata's resources were available if required and requested but not imposed. As Kant, managing director of the parent company, Tata Motors, explained: 'We are facilitators. We let local management run the business but we also have to come up with solutions.'

There was a series of contracts for the continuing supply of components and services from Ford. The terms of these varied – for engines, for example, supply was guaranteed through the life-cycle of current models and those in development, while other components were on rolling or renewable contracts. Most services were covered by an 18-month transitional agreement but Ford insisted that JLR must have a replacement for Ford Motor Credit in place within nine months.

JLR did not have sufficient resources to set up its own financial services business and so put the credit book out to tender to banks and other financial institutions. This was not a good time to be selling a portfolio covering the supply of premium cars to dealers worldwide and purchase arrangements with their retail customers. The main British banks were struggling to maintain their current positions and unwilling to bid. JLR asked for Tata's help and together they arrived at a regional solution, making deals with Chase Manhattan and J.P. Morgan for North America and FGAC, a joint venture between the Fiat Group and Crédit Agricole, for the UK and Europe. The latter would involve the revalidation of every wholesale dealer in Europe.

A transitional team drawn from the JLR executive committee also met with specialists from Tata Motors and other parts of the Tata Group to discuss possible areas of cooperation. Tata Consultancy Services was an early port of call, as JLR needed to overhaul and extend its IT system, not only to separate accounting and administration from Ford, but also for its expanding engineering and design functions.

A JLR team went to India to present its marketing and advertising programme, which, as well as setting the scene for selling Jaguars and Land Rovers in India, was of interest to Tata Motors because it had hitherto paid little attention to marketing its own products. There were lengthy discussions about manufacturing and purchasing from which it was agreed that there were opportunities for reducing the cost of tooling but not many possibilities for component sharing or technology transfer from JLR to Tata's own-brand vehicles.

Smith tackled the complex organisational issues with alacrity but didn't have the same experience or confidence when it came to product. He described the premium car business as 'a capital-intensive fashion industry' and said that Jaguar was 'on a path of resizing for a smaller volume', so prices and margins would need to be higher to generate the same revenue. This, he said later, was misinterpreted by reporters as Jaguar planning a steep move upmarket to compete with Bentley and Aston Martin, an idea also encouraged by Ratan Tata's hint that JLR might revive the Daimler name for a car beyond the Jaguar XJ.

It was clear, however, that the policy was to grow margins and revenue-per-car in the mature markets of Europe and North America, while increases in volume were to come from the new and emerging markets further afield. The Range Rover was already the top-selling luxury car in Russia, China was developing fast, and there were strong prospects elsewhere in Asia and in Latin America. And there was an obvious opportunity in India, where, pre-Tata, it sold fewer than 100 cars a year.

Smith became preoccupied with dealing with the UK government and the European Union, particularly in making an agreement with the latter on the upcoming legislation on carbon dioxide (CO_2) emissions.

As part of the European agreement to limit greenhouse gases, with the intention of mitigating the effects of global warming, manufacturers would have to achieve a fleet average for cars sold in Europe of less than 130 grammes per kilometre of carbon dioxide by 2012. CO_2 output is directly related to fuel consumption and so this looked difficult but attainable for the volume manufacturers selling a high proportion of small cars but impossible for a small company specialising in larger and heavier ones with big and powerful engines. It had not been a major concern for Ford as the relatively small number of Jaguars and Land Rovers could be offset against hundreds of thousands of Fiestas and Focuses but it posed a problem for JLR as a stand-alone business; its parent, Tata, did not have the prospect of selling enough small cars in Europe to make a difference.

Smith enlisted support from the UK government and British members of the European Parliament for flexibility on the CO_2 regulations. It helped that in Germany, Porsche – the only other independent car maker of similar size to JLR – was also lobbying for special arrangements. Eventually, the European Commission was persuaded that companies with sales in Europe of fewer than 300,000 a year should be allowed to make individual agreements equivalent to an overall 25 per cent CO_2 reduction compared with 2007.

The lightweight aluminium construction of the Jaguar XJ and XK was a good start but would need a wider application if JLR was to improve fuel efficiency across the whole range. In the last year of the Premier Automotive Group, Ford's chief technical officer, Richard Parry-Jones, had set up a development programme for an aluminium Range Rover and that car was part of the product plan that Tata inherited. To put it into production by 2013 would require significant investment in production facilities. A smaller Land Rover, exemplified by the LRX, made in higher volume, would also bring down the company's average fuel economy.

To meet these future challenges, the independent JLR would have to increase its research and development capability to a level disproportionate to its size and revenue. The annual R&D budget of £400 million was increased to more than £800 million, similar to that of much larger manufacturers – it had to be, for the cost of engineering is much the same whether 5,000 or 500,000 cars are produced. Smith was proud to proclaim that JLR accounted for 50 per cent of all the automotive R&D expenditure in the UK.

Developing and producing cars is a long-cycle business. Although some manufacturers claim that they have reduced the time from design approval to manufacture to 18 months, for most, bringing a new model from concept to reality takes about four years. Capricious markets, competition, and changing legislative requirements, dictate the time of model replacement – nowadays, usually after six years, although premium cars selling in smaller numbers can stay fresher for longer.

In this respect, Tata acquired JLR at a good time. The XF – the first Jaguar with twenty-first-century style – was launched just before the purchase was completed, a similarly mould-breaking XJ was ready, and the LRX was poised to expand Land Rover's horizons as the Range Rover Evoque.

2008 was heralded as the start of a new era for electric cars. Nissan was the trailblazer, promising that a plug-in small car (the Leaf) would be available within two years. Some US states were threatening to require manufacturers to sell a proportion of 'zero emissions' vehicles and so most of the volume manufacturers decided that they also should be ready with electric or petrol–electric hybrid models.

At JLR, Smith was excited about electrics and hybrids and the company became an enthusiastic participant in several government-backed development projects, the most prominent of which was Limo Green, an electric Jaguar XJ with a small petrol engine as a range-extender. At our meeting in July 2009, Smith said: 'Jaguar Land Rover will have at least two or three electric or hybrid vehicles in production within five years.' The first would be a hybrid version of the new Range Rover in 2013.

The author learned of Limo Green early in 2009 and drove the first prototype a year later, after the new XJ had broken cover. Jaguar led the consortium of companies which built this car with part-funding from the Technology Strategy Board, a UK government agency.

The idea of Limo Green was similar to the Chevrolet Volt which had recently been announced in America: a car driven by an electric motor, with the latest lithium-ion batteries that could be charged by plugging into the household mains or, when on a journey, by the petrol engine acting as an on-board generator. With fully charged batteries, it could run up to 50 mph and for 30 miles as a pure electric car, the 1.2 litre three-cylinder engine cutting in only when required for higher speeds or longer range.

Here was a long-wheelbase Jaguar XJ-L with the fuel economy of a small hatchback – 57 miles per gallon, a CO_2 figure approaching that of the much smaller Toyota Prius hybrid, acceleration as quick as the big diesel saloons from Audi, BMW and Mercedes, and a motorway cruising speed of 80 mph (130 km/h).

In 2010, as the first electric cars started to become available (officially encouraged by government grants, a policy that, in 2013, has yet to prove its worth), Limo Green appeared a promising solution to the problem of providing an ultra-low emissions official limousine. As the Jaguar XJ was the vehicle of choice for the British prime minister and his most senior cabinet colleagues, some at JLR were keen for Limo Green to progress to limited production; however, it didn't happen – Smith's successors were to have other priorities.

A low-carbon strategy was not only essential if JLR was to keep up with the leaders of the world motor industry, it was also a requirement if the company was to receive any support from the UK government. Funding for the Limo Green programme and associated projects on hybrids and lightweight aluminium vehicles depended on them fitting the environmental agenda.

These research projects – to which JLR pledged £800 million over five years – allowed the company to demonstrate to government the depth of its technology and emphasise Tata's commitment to manufacturing in the UK.

With the demise of Rover and the closure of Peugeot's Coventry plant, JLR was the only major car manufacturer left in the

Midlands, once famous throughout the world as Britain's industrial powerhouse. And as Ford stopped and General Motors reduced car production in the UK, JLR emerged as the country's largest automotive employer. The Japanese 'transplants' of Honda, Nissan and Toyota produced more cars but these companies conducted only a small proportion of their engineering work in the UK. JLR took every opportunity to remind the government that it employed 16,000 people, 3,500 of them in research and development.

For most of its 13 years in power, Britain's Labour administration showed scant interest in manufacturing and seemed to regard making cars as yesterday's industry. Although superficially supportive of JLR, the government remained suspicious and uncooperative when it came to money. Tata needed to fund the investment required for the JLR development plan to which it had agreed at the time of the takeover but became concerned as credit markets tightened.

Then, on 15 September 2008, investment bank Lehman Brothers filed for Chapter 11 bankruptcy protection in New York. With losses and bad debts amounting to hundreds of billions of dollars, it was the largest bankruptcy in US history and it led to disarray in the western world's banking industry and recession in the US and most countries in Europe.

With a major economic crisis coming so soon after the takeover, Jaguar Land Rover could not avoid the fallout.

9

Downturn

THE FINANCIAL CRISIS prompted by the Lehman crash might have changed everything at JLR. It certainly vindicated Ford's decision to sell the business to Tata rather than a private equity firm, which in the new fiscal climate would have been reluctant or unable to make the investment required to safeguard its future.

As the western world plunged towards recession, car makers saw their sales plummet. Consumers cut spending, and the more expensive premium models, always a discretionary purchase, sat forlornly in dealer showrooms. This had an unexpected effect with far-reaching consequences. As cars that previously would have been replaced routinely after two or three years were retained and lease agreements extended, owners discovered that cars last much longer and better than they did 20 years ago. Buying patterns, particularly those of big company fleets, altered – and will never be the same again.

The premium car market in the US fell by 50 per cent in just a few weeks. By the end of 2008, year-on-year global Jaguar sales were down some 30 per cent and Land Rover had dropped more than 35 per cent.

The last thing a manufacturer wants or can afford is to face the winter with stocks of unsold cars. At that stage, it was anyone's guess how much further markets would decline. In January 2009, David Smith and his management team took the decision – earlier than most – to cut production sharply, which meant losing 450 jobs and putting the Castle Bromwich, Halewood and Solihull plants on a four-day week. If this looked like Tata reneging on promises made at the time of the takeover – well, sorry, but the world had changed. The JLR business plan had to be rewritten.

The unions agreed to the job cuts, short-time working and a pay freeze in return for an assurance that there would be no more job losses for two years. This deal showed a welcome realism from the workforce but also reassurance from the company: however tough things were now, the plan was still for long-term growth.

JLR suffered more than its premium competitors in the financial storm. That was mostly because Audi, BMW and Mercedes were able to benefit from the fast-growing market in China, which was scarcely affected by this crisis of capitalism. They had all been in China for some time whereas Jaguar and Land Rover were only just beginning to gain traction there. And JLR was not yet properly established in India, another growing market area which was also largely insulated from the downturn.

In its homeland, Tata confirmed that it would keep faith with its new British acquisition. Speaking at Tata Group headquarters, Bombay House, Mumbai, in November 2008, just days before the massacre at the nearby (Tata-owned) Taj Mahal Palace Hotel, Ravi Kant reflected on JLR's sudden change of fortune:

The magnitude and speed of the meltdown took us by surprise. But Tata has 60 years' experience in the commercial vehicle business. We understand the cycles of the auto market and that the amplitude of those cycles changes from time to time. It is unfortunate that we encountered this difficult economic situation so soon after our acquisition but we are positive that we will come through it.

Back in Britain, there was a more immediate problem: cashflow. JLR would need to raise up to £800 million in the coming months but the banks had stopped lending. In November, Smith and his colleagues, followed by Ratan Tata himself, began a series of meetings with Lord Mandelson, the business secretary, to ask for help. The meetings were not fruitful. The official attitude seemed to be: why should the UK government provide access to funds for a rich Indian company, particularly when there was no financial crisis and recession in India? There was also an under-lying suspicion that, sooner or later, JLR production would be transferred to India, with the further loss of UK jobs.

Tata's troubles in the UK were not just with JLR. A steep drop in demand for steel products had forced Tata Steel to shut several British plants, laying off more than 5,000 staff. Wealthy or not, the Tata Group didn't have enough cash to take JLR through 2009, pending what it hoped would be a return to prof-itability in 2010.

Smith made an impassioned last-ditch plea to the govern-ment at a dinner of the Confederation of British Industry (CBI) in February 2009, which Mandelson attended. In his speech, he said that JLR had made a pre-tax profit of £600 million in the 18 months leading up to the credit crunch (under Ford and later Tata) but was now struggling with the impact of an unprec-edented financial crisis. There was an urgent need for support to 'avoid the industrial consequences of another quarter like this one'. He continued:

> What we want from the government is simply what we should be getting from those same banks who caused this crisis in the first place: short-term loans or loan guarantees to keep the wheels turning during the economic recession.

> I am pleased to see that in recent weeks the government has recognised this need and is prepared to take action, but we need it quickly and urgently to help manufacturing industry over the next few months.

The following month, Mandelson's grandly named Department for Business, Enterprise and Regulatory Reform (BERR) did agree to underwrite a £340 million three-year loan from the European Investment Bank (EIB). But before that money became available, JLR received another offer from BERR to guarantee £450 million in loans from RBS and Lloyds, two clearing banks which had been bailed out by the UK Treasury and were effectively under government control.

The details of that offer have never been made public but, on 1 May 2009, Tata issued this statement:

> The conditions demanded by BERR were so onerous that no public company with a fiduciary duty to its shareholders could have accepted them. The board of Tata Motors, owner of Jaguar Land Rover, has therefore been compelled to decline the terms demanded.

> Tata Motors is now reviewing the position of Jaguar Land Rover. Tata Motors has injected almost £900 million into Jaguar Land Rover over the past six months but could not

continue to support the company without loan finance from UK banks.

According to a usually well-informed analyst, Howard Wheeldon, then senior strategist at brokers BGC Partners, those BERR conditions included a seat on the JLR management board and the right to choose its chairman. With the power to veto investment and employment issues, that would, in effect, have given the government management control. Furthermore, the guarantee for the EIB loan was to be halved, reduced in term and subject to a substantial charge.

Wheeldon suggested that the rejected offer indicated a serious disagreement between BERR and the Treasury, with or without the involvement of Gordon Brown, prime minister and previously chancellor of the exchequer. Either way, he said:

> Tata appears to have been treated by the UK government as nothing more than a mere pawn in the future recovery and growth process of Jaguar Land Rover. Tata has been let down and could be excused for taking the whole business to India, lock, stock and barrel.

Interviewed by Dominic O'Connell, business editor of *The Sunday Times*, shortly after the stand-off, Ratan Tata was typically diplomatic but his annoyance and frustration showed through. He said:

> I would like to see the British government playing only one role. It controls the banks and all I seek is the facilitation to provide access to credit on commercial terms. It is not a bail-out.
>
> We are responsible for the fortunes of the company but this is a bone-dry situation in terms of access to credit. Nobody

can operate on that basis unless you have large cash balances, which we don't. My concern is that the government doesn't appear to care about manufacturing.

This was a critical point in Tata's ownership of JLR. It wasn't about to close it down or take the whole thing to India but it retreated from UK and European government-linked financial institutions and set about raising cash in India and from banks elsewhere.

Over the next few months, Tata secured over £500 million of funding for Jaguar Land Rover from the State Bank of India, Standard Chartered Bank, Bank of Baroda, ABC International Bank, GE Capital and Burdale Financial Limited of Ireland. And, by October 2009, Tata Motors had repaid and partly refinanced the $3 billion bridging loan for the JLR acquisition through a combination of a rights issue, cash and the issue of long maturity debentures, global depository shares and convertible notes.

JLR's progress with its product plan was somewhat overshadowed by the financial difficulties. In the first year of Tata's ownership, there had been a quiet revolution at Jaguar, signified by the emergence of the XF saloon.

Tata cannot take any credit for the XF, which was poised for launch when the Indian company was nominated as the favoured bidder for JLR. The decision finally to break away from Jaguar's traditional styling had been taken in Ford's time, when the company was headed by Geoff Polites, and it allowed design chief Ian Callum finally to demonstrate his vision for the marque.

Callum, a graduate of the respected automotive design course at the Royal College of Art in London, had always wanted to work for Jaguar. As a schoolboy, he wrote to Sir William Lyons saying that he wanted to be a car designer and he cites the encouraging reply he received as a main impetus for joining his chosen profession. On the way to his dream job he worked for Ford, TWR (Tom Walkinshaw Racing) and Aston Martin – all at some time associated with Jaguar – and his designs included the universally admired Aston Martin DB7 and Vanquish, the Ford Puma, and the Volvo C70 coupe and convertible. He was appointed Jaguar design chief (also retaining Aston Martin) in 1999, after the untimely death of Geoff Lawson, who had been 'head of styling' since the John Egan era.

While he had enjoyed the freedom of creating a new style for Aston Martin, Callum had found Jaguar obstinately conservative and he had been restricted to modifying the established designs of the XJ and S-Type. Even the new XK sports car, launched in 2006 and constructed in aluminium like the X350 XJ, had been like an evolution of the earlier, steel-bodied XK8. So when he presented the C-XF concept car at the 2007 Detroit Auto Show, Callum said: 'This is the Jaguar that has been in my head for eight years.'

As its name implied, the C-XF previewed the XF production model that was to appear for the first time at the Frankfurt Motor Show eight months later. The concept car was rather more extreme in its profile – acknowledging the Mercedes CLS 'four-door coupe' that had appeared a couple of years before – but the XF retained its aggressive, wedgy stance and showed a new face for Jaguar. The traditional four individual headlights and flush grille had been replaced by the latest in headlamp technology, twin lights combined under elongated covers, and a rectangular air intake with a sunken grille which carried the leaping cat motif.

The XF was, as one reviewer put it, the first Jaguar that didn't look like one. As well as bringing a new style, it indicated a new priority for the company. The replacement for the S-Type had been expected to follow the XJ and XK and be made in aluminium but Jaguar, at last, realised that modern styling and cabin furnishings were more likely to attract new customers than superior technology. The XF was, and is, based on a modified version of the steel platform that underpinned the S-Type and Lincoln LS a decade before.

There was no such reprieve for the Mondeo-based – and traditional looking – X-Type. The US dealers had never wanted a smaller and cheaper Jaguar and greeted the X-Type with little enthusiasm. Unsold cars meant that discounting followed, which wasn't good for Jaguar's image, and early in 2008, when the pound–dollar exchange rate became particularly unfavourable, the decision was taken to withdraw the X-Type from the US market.

Production, which had never met Ford's expectations, was halved by the loss of US sales and the general slump elsewhere, so the X-Type's days were numbered. In July 2009, the Tata-owned business decided to cut its losses and announced the end of X-Type production. That would mean 300 redundancies at Halewood.

The Merseyside factory was promised the LRX to take the X-Type's place alongside the Land Rover Freelander 2 but the new model would not be ready until 18 months after the last X-Type came off the line in December.

The Land Rover LRX concept followed a year behind the Jaguar C-XF, at the 2008 Detroit Auto Show. It was the work of Gerry McGovern, design director of Land Rover since 2006.

Although McGovern is smooth, polished and expensively tailored in his middle age (for years, he had unfashionably long hair), he is, as Ford creative director J Mays once put it, 'steeped in Land Rover DNA'. He had designed the Freelander at Rover

Ratan Tata, chairman of Tata Sons, was the driving force in the purchase of Jaguar Land Rover.

Ravi Kant, managing
director of Tata
Motors 2005-2009.

Tata Motors has a
campus-style factory
complex in Pune.

Tata presented the Indica (centre) in 1998 as the Indian national car.
In 2003, it signed a contract with MG-Rover to supply a version of the
Indica V2 as the CityRover (below).

By 2008, the Tata Indica had evolved into the Vista, sold alongside the Nano (left), the world's cheapest new car.

Ratan Tata (left) and Ravi Kant with the electric Indica EV, developed at the Tata Motors Technical Centre at Warwick University, UK.

Wolfgang Reitzle, chairman of Rover under BMW, became the first president of Ford's Premier Automotive Group.

The third-generation Range Rover, code-named L322, was Reitzle's baby, developed by BMW and launched by Ford.

Jaguar's only venture into Formula 1 was notably unsuccessful in five seasons of racing.

Technical breakthrough – in 2002 the shiny Jaguar XJ heralded JLR aluminium body construction.

First Range Rover Sport shared its chassis with Discovery and became Land Rover's highly profitable best-seller.

Mark Fields was president of Premier Automotive Group on his way to Ford second in command.

Lewis Booth followed Fields at PAG but had to preside over the sale of Jaguar and Land Rover.

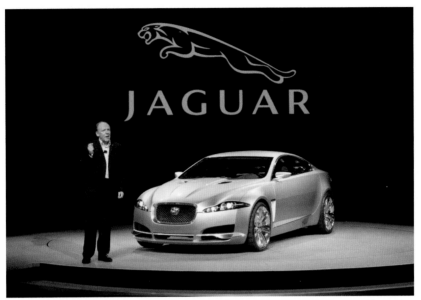

The C-XF concept car, presented by Ian Callum at the Detroit Auto Show in 2007, showed a new style for Jaguar.

In Detroit a year later, the Land Rover LRX concept gained critics' approval. It became the Range Rover Evoque.

Alan Mulally produced a remarkable turnround at Ford but cast aside its European premium brands.

Handover – JLR chief executive David Smith with Lewis Booth (left) and Ratan Tata at the signing ceremony at Gaydon, 2 June 2008.

and worked for Land Rover through the BMW days before heading Ford's Lincoln studio in the US, and returning to Land Rover as director of advanced design in 2004.

LRX was an exercise to see how far Land Rover could be extended. Could it compete in the emerging market for SUV crossovers and retain the peerless off-road ability for which its products were world renowned? Though it was far from its natural habitat, the coupe-like LRX scored a hit amongst the bruiser American SUVs in Detroit and it was received with similar enthusiasm at its subsequent motor show appearances.

One of Tata's earliest decisions for JLR was to approve LRX for production. The concept was supposed to be a diesel–electric hybrid but, once again, it was the shape and style that caught the public's interest. With a conventional powertrain, LRX could be built on the same platform as the Freelander. LRX wouldn't be on sale (as the Range Rover Evoque) until the end of 2011. In the meantime, Land Rover could do no more than freshen its current range and make some changes to the engine line-up.

There was a hint of desperation in presenting these as 2010 models in April 2009. The Range Rover and Range Rover Sport were given the improved 5 litre V8 petrol engine, which was also introduced in the Jaguar XF and XJ. The Sport also offered the revised 3 litre V6 diesel engine from the XF. The Discovery had the biggest visual change, losing its unadorned 'industrial' look in favour of a softer style with a bright grille and sparkly LED lights, like the Range Rovers. The American market had dismissed the Discovery (then called LR3 in the US) as 'not premium enough'. The shiny, facelifted and refurnished model was christened Discovery 4 (LR4 in America) and was to have a new lease of life when the markets started to pick up again.

But as 2009 wore on, with no sign of an improvement in economic conditions, sales continued to decline. David Smith reflected that he had come into a company that was profitable and growing and was now in charge of one with sales at a ten-year low. He could only hope for better times ahead.

10

The boys from BMW

IN RETROSPECT, TATA DID WELL to avoid government involvement in the finances of Jaguar Land Rover. The upturn, when it came, showed Tata and JLR to be stronger on their own. They could resist political pressures but also had some leverage for grants and assistance for their expansion plans. There were some similarities, on a smaller scale, to Ford in America, which remained aloof from the government bail-outs for General Motors and Chrysler and recovered from the downturn more quickly as a result.

But early in 2009 the prospects had not seemed bright. The Jaguar XF had been well reviewed and was attracting new customers – but not enough of them. Once again, Ford planners had missed the main part of the market. The XF offered a diesel engine but it was a 2.7 litre V6, while most sales of the rival BMW 5 series and Mercedes E-Class were more frugal four-cylinder models.

Land Rover was facing renewed hostility from the anti-SUV brigade who sought to shame owners of large, thirsty four-wheel drive vehicles for using them on the urban school run and other activities that didn't require their cross-country abilities. Sharply increased fuel prices and the UK introduction in 2005 of tiered vehicle excise duty based on carbon dioxide output had already penalised Range Rover and Discovery owners and London mayor Ken Livingstone had threatened to impose a £25 a day congestion charge on vehicles with a CO_2 rating above 225 g/km. To appease the environmentalists, Land Rover added a carbon-offset payment to the price of each car sold in the UK and some other European countries but it had no immediate answer to those who condemned their products as overweight and over-qualified for the way most were used.

For a while, it looked as if the 'buy-one-and-get-one-free' deal accepted by Tata a year before had been turned on its head: Jaguar was on a rise, albeit only a slight incline, and Land Rover, the consistent money-spinner, was on the back foot. Overall, sales were still in decline. The naysayers of the takeover preened themselves: Tata had paid too much at the wrong time and would have to curtail its ambitions.

Sure enough, after 18 months of non-interference, Tata appointed KPMG International and Roland Berger Strategy Consultants to study cost reductions at JLR as part of a strategic review.

The result, when it became known in September 2009, was a plan to close one of the three JLR factories by 2014. This news was accompanied by a new pay and pensions package for its production units. In common with most UK businesses, it proposed to close its final salary pension scheme to new entrants. New staff would be paid 20 per cent less than existing personnel but there was a guarantee that the jobs of 8,000 full-time staff (more than half the workforce) would be secure until 2015.

Although the company had warned that the business plan agreed at the time of the takeover would have to be revised to reflect the new economic conditions, the unions were immediately opposed to these proposals. Negotiations continued through the end of the year but broke down in January.

David Smith's position was clearly weakened by the failure to reach agreement, so the announcement, on 25 January 2010, that he was leaving the company was not entirely unexpected. No explanation was given but the buzz around the industry was that a space was being created for Carl-Peter Forster, who had resigned as president of General Motors Europe two months earlier.

Smith's departure signalled the major change in JLR top management that some observers had advocated from the start of Tata's takeover. The most successful premium car companies are German and BMW represented the business model that Tata wanted to emulate with JLR. Several of BMW's most prominent and accomplished senior managers had left the company in the wake of its Rover debacle, nine years before. Forster was one.

Forster, urbane but sharply analytical in business, had been tipped for the top job at BMW but, as director of manufacturing, disagreed with its board about the direction for Rover. General Motors was quick to take him on, as head of its European operations and chairman of Opel and Saab. All went well for a while but by 2009 GM in America was heading for bankruptcy and the board of directors decided that it must discard its loss-making overseas subsidiaries.

That course of action was clear when Forster used the Opel press conference at the 2009 Geneva Motor Show not so much to sell its new products as to hawk the company itself to potential investors. Tata's Ravi Kant sensed Forster's discomfort and invited him to breakfast at a Geneva hotel the following day. At that meeting, Kant – who was due to retire as Tata Motors managing director later in the year – asked if he would be interested in heading Tata Motors and therefore its wholly owned subsidiary, Jaguar Land Rover. Intrigued by the prospect, Forster met Ratan Tata later the same day. They got on well and agreed to stay in touch as the Opel sale process progressed.

Forster engaged in negotiations to sell Opel to a consortium led by component and contract car manufacturer Magna and two Russian banks, but his position became untenable when a new General Motors board, appointed after its 'quickie' Chapter 11 bankruptcy, decided to keep its European subsidiary after all. Any doubts he had about Tata's offer were dispelled. In February 2010, it was announced that Forster had been appointed chief executive of Tata Motors and chairman of Jaguar Land Rover.

In parallel, David Smith was replaced as JLR chief executive by Ralf Speth, also German and also schooled at BMW. Speth had last served BMW as vice president of Land Rover, transferred to Ford's Premier Automotive Group as director of production, quality and product planning and right-hand man to Wolfgang Reitzle, and later moved to the German industrial group Linde, where Reitzle had been appointed chairman and chief executive.

Speth had studied for his doctorate at Warwick University under Professor Lord Bhattacharyya, who was pleased to recommend him to Ratan Tata and Ravi Kant. Bhattacharyya described Speth as 'a passionate engineer with German discipline who understands the British'. Speth had the advantage of knowing and having worked with many of the incumbent JLR management and, importantly, had been responsible for commonality between the brands when he was at PAG.

Forster and Speth were all smiles when they appeared for the first time in public as the two most senior JLR executives at the

Geneva Motor Show in March 2010, exactly a year after Tata's first approach to Forster. The nervousness and uncertainty among the existing JLR people was palpable; clearly, it was no longer going to be business as usual.

The author had dinner with Forster on the eve of the show, just a few days into his new job. It was too early for him to detail plans for Tata or JLR but his objectives were clear: Jaguar and Land Rover needed to sell more cars and make more money and the Tata brand should evolve as a maker of innovative, high-quality vehicles that could be sold across the world. He found the entrepreneurial spirit at Tata refreshing after the restrictions and bureaucracy of General Motors and likened it more to the atmosphere at BMW. Most of all, he had confidence in Tata's long-term vision: 'In my experience, if you take the short-term view you are always in trouble.'

He was also acutely aware of the parallels between Tata's ownership of JLR and the way that BMW mishandled Rover in the early days. In both cases, the new owners initially left the previous management in place and didn't intervene in the running of the business. The arrival of Forster and Speth was equivalent to Reitzle moving in to shake up Rover, 15 years before.

Forster was born in the UK, the son of a German diplomat. He trained in economics and as an aerospace engineer in Germany and worked in the McKinsey management consultancy before joining BMW in 1986 and quickly moving up the ranks to the board of management. Now, for the first time since childhood, he was moving his home to England and would split his time between JLR and Tata in India.

One of Forster's first appointments was another ex-BMW colleague, Tim Leverton, as engineering chief in India, responsible for developing the future range of Tata cars and trucks. Leverton had worked at BMW-owned Rover and transferred to Rolls-Royce Motors when it was acquired by BMW. He was responsible for the Rolls-Royce Phantom before moving to the industrial and agricultural vehicle maker, JCB. Among his responsibilities there was the JCB Dieselmax, which broke a series of world speed records for diesel-powered cars driven by Land Speed record holder, Andy Green.

The new chairman also brought in Frank Klaas as JLR head of communications. A former business journalist, and successful racing driver, Klaas had been in charge of communications and public relations at Opel and General Motors Europe.

Talking to the press in Geneva just after he and Speth had arrived at JLR, Forster asked for 100 days to get to know the business and promised to outline their plans soon after that. True to his word, three months later, the day after Tata Motors issued its results for the year ending 31 March 2010, Forster and Speth briefed business journalists at a breakfast meeting in the Radisson Edwardian Hotel at Heathrow Airport. They had just stepped off a plane from Mumbai, after attending the most important board meeting in JLR's short history under Tata's ownership.

They were able to report that sales had improved since the turn of the year – indeed, March 2010 had been Land Rover's best-ever month in the UK – and there had been a financial turnround. Jaguar Land Rover had made a pre-tax profit of £32 million – not a lot, but a move in the right direction.*

Forster described a new strategy based on three brands: Jaguar, Land Rover and Range Rover. Establishing the latter as

---

*The pre-tax profit for 2009–2010 was later quoted as £51 million. The apparent discrepancy is explained by a change from Tata's GAAP (Generally Accepted Accounting Principles) figure to the IFRS (International Financial Reporting Standards) calculation used by JLR.

a separate brand was seen as a big opportunity. The key was the decision to present the Land Rover LRX as a Range Rover and price it accordingly. Forster and Speth had great hopes for this car, which would go into production in 2011 (as the Evoque). Their optimism was not misplaced but the idea of separating Range Rover from Land Rover was eventually rejected.

Separate or together, with Range Rover spanning price and size classes from LRX to the Sport and the 'full size' Range Rover, Forster suggested that there was room for a fourth, mid-size model above the LRX.

He confirmed that the next top-model Range Rover would have an aluminium structure like the Jaguar XJ and XK but indicated that a new basic Land Rover to replace the Defender was still work-in-progress: 'We don't yet know how to do it. The vehicle that was planned is too expensive. We have to take some cost out.'

The emphasis at Jaguar was on expanding the range with a sports car priced below the XK and another smaller model, but Forster would not elaborate on the type or when it would be introduced.

To meet forthcoming European Union emissions standards, it was clear that it would need more small-displacement four-cylinder engines as well as the 3 litre V6 engine derived from the 5 litre V8 made for JLR by Ford at Bridgend. To the surprise of those attending, Forster said that JLR would design its own 2 litre four-cylinder engines, petrol and diesel, suitable for front-, rear- and four-wheel drive vehicles – and, in different form, also applicable to Tata's own products. At that stage, there was no information about where these engines would be built but a clear hint that at least some would be made in India.

This was all positive stuff: having solved its funding problems and appointed a management team of world-class Germans,

Tata was showing JLR a direction for the future, based on investment for growth rather than cost-cutting to balance the books.

Examination of the accounts showed that this was a brave strategy to spell out at that moment. Although there was an upturn at the time they were issued, the production figures for the past year as a whole were far lower than anyone expected: 146,564 for Land Rover and 47,418 for Jaguar. That was a 33 per cent drop on 286,880 combined sales for calendar year 2007 – the figure which had loomed large in the takeover negotiations.

Forster knew from bitter experience not to make volume predictions but it was understood that the first priority was to get back to around 300,000 units. He did say that JLR expected further export growth, especially in the Chinese market, which was expanding at more than 30 per cent a year.

JLR realised that eventually it would have to form a joint venture with a Chinese partner for local production. And, in view of Tata's ownership, it obviously wanted to promote sales in India. Local assembly would also be needed there but Forster and Speth were quick to point out that didn't mean taking business away from the UK factories; they would actually make more cars, exported as CKD (Completely Knocked Down) kits.

The future of those UK factories – at Castle Bromwich, Halewood and Solihull – was the next big issue for JLR's new management.

11

Reorganisation, new spirit

B Y AUTO INDUSTRY STANDARDS, three vehicle assembly
plants is at least one too many for a company the size of
Jaguar Land Rover. The conventional wisdom is that 200,000 is
a minimum annual production for a single plant and, by 2010,
JLR had never reached more than 300,000 from three.

It was clear to Carl-Peter Forster – who had experience of
UK car factories in a previous role as manufacturing director
of BMW and Rover – that JLR would be better off with just two
manufacturing locations. This issue had been simmering since
the previous September and was a serious bone of contention
with the unions, who had still not come to an agreement with
the company over pay and conditions.

At a briefing in May 2010, Forster said:

The future products for both brands will be built on a more
modular system [a reference to aluminium construction which

would spread from Jaguar to the 2013 Range Rover], so making them in one large plant would be more efficient than in two smaller ones.

Logically, that one plant would be in the Midlands – either Castle Bromwich or Solihull, which are just 10 miles (16 km) apart – and the betting was on the former, as Solihull needed modernisation and sits on more valuable land. Halewood, on Merseyside, 120 miles (190 km) further north, would continue to build the smaller and more conventional models.

The plant closure issue was still on the table when Forster talked to journalists at the Paris Motor Show in October. He claimed his motives were misunderstood, that the ambition was to produce more vehicles and employ more people in the UK, and that there was no intention to reduce JLR's total direct workforce of 16,000. The move should be seen not as closing a factory but as a merger, creating one larger plant from two. Forster said: 'Technically, the decision has been made: the two operations should merge.' But, he added, JLR management was still open to discussing alternatives.

Just two weeks later, JLR announced that it would keep all three factories open.

How much the threat of consolidation was a tactic in the long-running negotiations about pay and conditions at the Midlands factories is still a matter of debate. Some people close to JLR maintain that plant closure was never an option and in any case would have been unacceptable politically; at the time of the takeover, Tata had pledged to keep the factories and workforce intact. Others believe that both Castle Bromwich and Solihull survived because there was, at last, a settlement of the labour dispute. The unions agreed to a deal which gave a 5 per cent pay rise the following month (November) and a further 3 per cent in

November 2011, with lower rates for new hires and lower shift premiums.

Some outsiders saw the retention of both Midlands factories as a missed opportunity for rationalisation and cost-saving. Before the takeover, Ford anticipated making all the aluminium-bodied cars in one plant and JLR's local management followed the same logic. It was clear that, in the changed economic climate, continuing with three plants would only be viable as part of a seriously ambitious expansion plan.

By the autumn of 2010, JLR was seeing strong sales growth and the full-year figures would show combined sales of Jaguar and Land Rover at 232,839, up 19 per cent on 2009. But now equalling its previous best of 300,000 cars a year would not be enough: JLR would have to go way beyond that. At that time, not many observers gave it much chance of reaching 400,000; however, within two years that figure would look entirely possible, and 500,000 within reach.

The most significant sales increases in 2010 were in the UK (64 per cent), the United States (24 per cent) and China, where the JLR figures were double those of the previous year.

Forster knew that if the Chinese market kept growing – as everyone expected – JLR would reach a critical point, when it would not be able to keep pace unless it could offer cars at lower prices. Import duty and other taxes could more than double the price of an imported luxury car and while that did not hurt sales of the top Range Rover (the more expensive the better for China's super-rich), it made lesser models sold to the developing middle class uncompetitive.

In a speech to the British Society of Motor Manufacturers and Traders in June, Forster predicted: 'The gravitational pull to the east will be one of the dominant features of the next few years. We may look back on 2010 as the turning point.'

In other words, JLR had decided that it had to build cars in China.

Jaguar and Land Rover had only been in China (selling through four separate importers) since 2004 and wouldn't set up its own sales company in Shanghai until August 2011. JLR's rivals had been making cars there for some time. Audi, part of the Volkswagen Group, was firmly established as the leading premium brand, supplying official cars to the Chinese government as well as to the country's burgeoning industries (most of which are government-controlled). As the majority of the more expensive cars are chauffeur-driven, Audi, BMW and Cadillac made specially lengthened models in China to provide more rear-seat leg room.

A foreign car manufacturer intending to sell in the domestic market could not set up on its own in China; the government insisted on a 50:50 joint venture with a Chinese firm and had to give its approval for any such enterprise.

In autumn 2010, a task force of JLR executives went to China to visit a number of possible partners. The China project had been made more complicated by a new edict from the authorities: any new venture to build foreign cars must also include joint development with the approved partner of a new domestic brand. Even if the task force decided quickly on an associate, starting up in China was going to be a long process.

The new Jaguar XJ was the first JLR car designed with China in mind. The poor response of traditional markets to the previous XJ had prompted the complete and dramatic change of style but the extra chrome fittings, inside and out, were added to meet the tastes of clientele in the world's fastest-growing market.

July 2009, when the new XJ had been previewed to a celebrity audience at the Saatchi Gallery in London, was not the best of times for JLR. It was perhaps fortuitous that component supply problems delayed the XJ sales launch until spring 2010, when the company's fortunes were improving.

The publicity blurb declared that, with the XJ launch, 'the Jaguar renaissance is complete'. Design chief Ian Callum said that this car, rather than the XF, established the new look for the marque. Its long, low, swept-back shape and aggressive (Callum prefers 'assertive') gaping mouth were more extreme, and more distinctive, than the XF. The XJ was resolutely modern, confident; perhaps even a bit flash. The dwindling number of traditional Jaguar enthusiasts would probably hate it but that was the point: it was designed to appeal to buyers who would never previously have considered a Jaguar.

The Chinese – and other markets where such cars are predominantly chauffeur-driven – appreciated that a long-wheelbase XJ-L model was part of the concept, rather than an awkwardly stretched afterthought. Externally, the long and short XJs are hard to distinguish and Jaguar had ensured that there would be nothing to choose between them in performance and road behaviour.

Underneath its stylish new gown, the new XJ was not so different from the old one. That, it was generally agreed, was no bad thing. The previous X350's aluminium body structure was state-of-the-art, even if its exterior design wasn't. Although the new car was bigger – similar in size to the Audi A8, BMW 7 series and Mercedes S-Class – it was still 150–200 kg lighter than every one of its rivals. And, this time, Jaguar offered an appropriate diesel engine from the start; the 3 litre V6 XJ diesel was praised for its refinement and performance and would be the most popular version for Europe.

The 3 litre diesel, a new development by Jaguar of the V6 engine from an alliance between Ford and Peugeot, was introduced in the XF in mid 2009 – to the consternation of those who had bought the inferior 2.7 litre XF diesel only a year before. At the same time, the AJV8 petrol engine that had been made by Ford in Bridgend since 1996 was replaced by a more advanced 5 litre V8. These two new engines became JLR's mainstays for the bigger vehicles of both brands – and confirmed the continuity of supply from Ford for at least another generation.

With all its new products out in the market, Jaguar kept the publicity machine running with a surprise exhibit at the autumn motor shows in Paris and Los Angeles. The C-X75, so named to celebrate 75 years of Jaguar design (going back to the 1935 SS) was a flight of fancy that also made a statement about Jaguar's commitment to technological innovation.

Ian Callum and Julian Thompson, the head of Jaguar's advanced design studio, had produced a truly beautiful super-sports car that looked fit to rival the Bugatti Veyron or Ferrari Enzo but boasted a hybrid powertrain with four electric motors and two tiny gas turbines as electricity generators. C-X75 captured headlines when it was unveiled in Paris but made a bigger splash when a few journalists were invited to drive it at Santa Monica airport on the eve of the Los Angeles Auto Show.

The covers of motoring magazines screamed: 'We drive the world's first jet-powered supercar' and 'The Jaguar that can out-drag a Veyron', and their stories were peppered with tantalising statistics: 780 horsepower, maximum speed 205 mph (330 km/h), acceleration 0–62 mph (100 km/h) in 3.4 seconds.

All of this was feasible – and, indeed, the information was supplied by Jaguar – but none of it was actually true. The C-X75 show car was powered by nothing more sophisticated than an electric motor from a golf-cart. Its top speed was perhaps as high as 30 mph (50 km/h).

At that stage, C-X75 was no more than an exercise in shape and style, designers' self-indulgence. At a briefing in the car museum owned by Jay Leno, American chat show host and arch car enthusiast, Callum described it thus: 'C-X75 is as close to a pure art form as a concept car can get.'

The engineers in Jaguar's advanced technology department were working on hybrid solutions that included the gas turbine generators that lurked intriguingly but inoperably under C-X75's rear window. The micro-turbines were built by Bladon Jets, a small business started by a group of motorcycle racers, and, although they were not destined for production in C-X75 or any other car, they impressed Tata's technical team in the UK, who encouraged Tata to take a 20 per cent interest in the company.

C-X75 had done its job: a dream car that drew attention to Jaguar, an optimistic symbol for the marque's future. It wasn't expected, or intended, to go any further. But within JLR management there was a small group who thought that Jaguar should build a car like this, a high-technology supercar made in small numbers and sold at an appropriately high price to wealthy enthusiasts. Evidently, Ratan Tata also liked the idea, as Carl-Peter Forster came back from a board meeting in India in December and asked JLR engineering director, Bob Joyce, to find a way of turning the C-X75 into a production car.

The go-ahead was announced to the outside world the following May, just as Tata Motors presented its results for 2010/2011, showing a £1.15 billion profit for JLR.

The financial result vindicated the company's decision to maintain investment through the downturn. Ralf Speth could say with some pride that JLR was back on track, the new model plan was stabilised, and not only had it been decided to keep all three plants open but their full utilisation was in sight. JLR needed to recruit 1,000 extra engineers to work on the next generation of products and 1,500 assembly line personnel at

Halewood, where the Range Rover Evoque was being prepared for the sales launch in the autumn.

Jaguar introduced the facelifted XF, which was accompanied – at last – by a 2.2 litre four-cylinder diesel engine. This was a version of the engine already used in the Land Rover Freelander 2, adapted to Jaguar's different under-bonnet layout. This smaller diesel would become Jaguar's best-selling model in Europe.

The Evoque and this new version of the XF followed the trend of downsizing. All around the industry, car makers were adopting smaller engines, replacing V8s with V6s, and V6s with four-cylinder units. This achieved lower fuel consumption and reduced CO_2, while more advanced technology meant that there need be no loss of performance. Ford was one of the earliest proponents of downsizing, on both sides of the Atlantic, and JLR was able to use its own version of the Ford EcoBoost petrol engine in the Evoque and Freelander.

Ford continued to build all the engines for Jaguar and Land Rover but had made it clear at the time of the takeover that it would not do so indefinitely. There had been speculation about an alternative source of supply but, as JLR's volumes increased, the idea of setting up its own engine manufacturing plant became more attractive. In September 2011, it announced a £355 million investment in an engine plant to be built near Wolverhampton, in the West Midlands. It will make JLR-designed four-cylinder petrol and diesel engines and is expected to be up and running in 2014.

Carl-Peter Forster had referred to this engine programme 18 months earlier but he would not be at JLR to see its fruition. Suddenly and unexpectedly, it was announced on 9 September that Forster had ceased to be the group chief executive of Tata Motors. The statement said that he had stepped down due to 'unavoidable personal circumstances'; an illness in his family required him to be in Europe for more time than his commitments in India would allow.

Forster was not replaced directly. Ravi Kant, who had been appointed non-executive vice chairman of Tata Motors on his retirement, took back some of his old responsibilities. Ralf Speth's position as chief executive of JLR was unchanged; he had already been appointed to the Tata Motors board of directors.

Speth was clearly in charge when he talked to journalists at the Frankfurt Motor Show. Commenting on the hybrid power unit in the Jaguar C-X16 concept car, he said that JLR had established a research group at the University of Warwick to work on electric and hybrid power systems and it had concluded that, for the future, 'in the premium segment, hybrid is the best solution'. He also talked about the changing nature of the Defender market and how the two versions of Land Rover's DC100 concept demonstrated ways of providing a vehicle that could be used for both work and leisure.

On the Frankfurt show stand, between the Jaguar and Land Rover displays, was a bold sign with the letters 'JLR'. The industry understood it – as will readers of this book – but the general public were confused. It was the first and last appearance for this corporate logo. In the eyes of the outside world, the two car brands were all that mattered.

12

One company, two brands

Part of Ralf Speth's job when he was with Ford's Premier Automotive Group was to encourage engineering commonality between its member companies. By the time that Ford was preparing to dispose of Jaguar and Land Rover – and Speth had gone off to become chief operating officer at Linde – the integration of the two marques had reached a level that made it logical to sell them together, rather than individually.

Not long before, PAG's product development had been a mess. It was dealing with too many model programmes, using too many different platforms and components picked from around the Ford world. Richard Parry-Jones, then Ford's chief technical officer, began a process of rationalisation and, by 2008, current and future Jaguars and Land Rovers shared engines, electronics, safety systems and much else besides.

The Jaguar X-Type and the Land Rover Freelander were made in the same plant, at Halewood, and the (then undeclared) plan was for the next Range Rover to be built alongside the similarly aluminium-bodied Jaguar XJ and XK at Castle Bromwich. Jaguar and Land Rover back-office functions were mostly one and the same.

Two areas remained resolutely brand-specific – design, and sales and marketing. Jaguar and Land Rover each had their own design staff, with separate studios, at Whitley and Gaydon respectively. The Jaguar and Land Rover managing directors were, in effect, brand managers, primarily responsible for marketing, sales and service.

The JLR to which Speth had returned was, in world automotive terms, a small company with two complementary brands. It was essential to maintain the integrity of those brands – and therefore to preserve the autonomy of the design studios – but, as JLR entered and developed in new markets around the world, it made sense to have a unified sales operation.

With experience of managing portfolios of brands at PAG and Linde, Speth devised a new management structure for JLR. All operational decisions are now made through the executive committee, which meets at Whitley for an hour every Monday morning. Most of its members have glass-fronted offices opening on to a spacious lounge and meeting area on the first floor of the executive building opposite the Whitley engineering centre; JLR moved its headquarters there from Gaydon in October 2011. The office design, with its cool, glass-and-chrome furnishings, was specified by Land Rover's Gerry McGovern in his parallel role as chief creative officer.

The executive committee has 18 members representing all of the company's activities; in total, 20 managers report to Speth directly. This flat organisational structure eliminates one layer of management from the previous pyramid system, and is designed to reduce bureaucracy and speed up decision-making.

It is, incidentally, similar to that adopted by Jac Nasser when he was heading Ford and now used by Sergio Marchionne in running Fiat and Chrysler.

The ultimate authority at Jaguar Land Rover remains with the board of directors, which, in 2012, included Ratan Tata, Cyrus Mistry, deputy chairman of Tata Sons, and Andrew Robb from Tata Steel (who is the chairman of the company's audit committee). But this now acts more in the role of a supervisory board, in the German pattern, and meets quarterly. As a director of Tata Motors, Speth travels to India every 6–8 weeks to report on JLR's performance at its board meetings in Mumbai.

Speth, small in stature with longish, wavy black hair, a distinctive moustache and a warm smile, has a rather different persona from his compatriots who have held the top job. Wolfgang Reitzle projected a steely authority and Carl-Peter Forster had a diplomatic charm but both liked to be seen to be in charge. Speth is quiet and understated, and prefers those directly responsible for the cars and the brands to be the public face of the company. His bosses at Tata seem to like this approach, perhaps because they similarly eschew the cult of personality.

Speth's management restructure saw Phil Popham, managing director of Land Rover since 2006, promoted to a new role as director of global sales and service operations, responsible for both brands. To ensure that Jaguar and Land Rover each retained their identity and product attributes, two new global brand directors were appointed: Adrian Hallmark for Jaguar and John Edwards for Land Rover. Significantly, they joined the executive committee along with their design directors, Ian Callum and Gerry McGovern. Speth emphasises that this shows that the brands themselves are not integrated: 'We are one company, two brands.'

Popham's task was to build the linkage between the brands that was already established in some sales areas. As of 2012,

JLR was present in 177 countries. Mark Fields, as chairman of PAG, had introduced a strategy of combining the sales operations of its brands as they spread into new markets: some were Jaguar with Land Rover and others, as in Russia, Land Rover in conjunction with Volvo. In the United States, following PAG's ill-advised migration to California ten years before, Jaguar and Land Rover were run as one from the former Jaguar headquarters at Mahwah, New Jersey.

As part of the separation from Ford, JLR had set up new integrated sales companies in 25 export markets but they still provided separate dealer contracts for Jaguar and Land Rover. Very few of its dealers sold both from the same site. And, unusually for a motor manufacturer, neither Jaguar nor Land Rover owned any retail dealers.

It was decided that in future, where appropriate, newly appointed dealers would handle both brands. The two model ranges were, and would remain, complementary, in the same premium sector but with very different products at each size and price level. As more new models were introduced it was anticipated that the combined offer would be equal in scope to Audi, BMW or Mercedes.

Over the years, British car manufacturers, like other exporters, have been bedevilled by fluctuating exchange rates. On several occasions, Jaguar's very existence has been threatened by the relative strengths of sterling and the US dollar. More recently, local politics, taxes, economic crises, and even natural disasters, had put markets in turmoil and business at risk. JLR determined that it would work towards a more balanced future by dividing its sales operations into six regions, none of which should account for more than 20 per cent of the total revenue, profit or volume. The six regions are: United Kingdom, North America, China, Asia Pacific (excluding China), Europe (excluding the UK) and 'Overseas', encompassing Russia, the Middle East and Africa, and India.

It is clear that China will have to be an exception to the new rule. JLR's sales of imported cars (approximately 70,000 in 2012) already amounted to nearly 20 per cent of the total. Building cars there will mean significant additional volume for the region but the profits will be shared with JLR's joint venture partner, Chery.

Today, all eyes are on China, which since 2009 has been the world's largest car market, but for 60 years the most important export destination for Jaguar has been the United States. At its peak (2002), Jaguar sold more cars in the US than its total production in 2012. Land Rover, which didn't enter the US market officially until 1987, never had the same dependence on sales in America but it is still the biggest market in the world for Range Rover. New York City accounts for more Range Rover sales than any other single territory.

While they sit together in some of the multi-franchise mega-dealers, Jaguar and Land Rover have developed very differently in the US. Jaguar was established as a sophisticated metropolitan brand but when Land Rover arrived, with only one product (the Range Rover), it needed to do something different and established lodge-style Land Rover sales sites with off-road driving courses and an emphasis on leisure pursuits and 'the great outdoors'. Reconciling these two approaches is a job for Andy Goss, a former head of Porsche UK, who was appointed president of Jaguar Land Rover North America in April 2011.

The company had to recognise that, in some parts of the world, Jaguar and Land Rover didn't sit together very comfortably. That was one reason for the idea, articulated by Carl-Peter Forster early in his time as JLR chairman, of establishing Range Rover as a distinct third brand. This was a subject of serious discussion through 2010, as the reach of the Range Rover marque was about to be extended with the Evoque. The Land Rover faction was opposed to the separation, arguing that Range Rover should represent Land Rover at its best and be proud of sharing the versatility and off-road capability of its more utilitarian sibling. There were also practical considerations: at a time when JLR was working towards closer integration, a separate Range Rover would require its own dealer agreements.

Finally, it was agreed to maintain the status quo: 'together but separate'. Dealers already had signs with 'Range Rover' spelt out beneath the Land Rover oval. To reinforce the togetherness, advertisements were devised showing the Evoque alongside an original Land Rover and the launch promotion for the new full-size Range Rover carried the message: 'It's in the blood … our vehicles will always be Land Rover at heart.' When the Evoque first appeared it had no Land Rover identification, but for 2013 a small green oval badge was fixed to the front grille.

With this clarified, Popham's team commissioned a design blueprint for a showroom with the right environment to exhibit Jaguars and Land Rovers together. It was accepted, though, that local conditions and preferences would mean that, in some cases, one would have more prominence.

Under previous owners, Jaguar and Land Rover had paid little heed to the particular demands of local markets. Gary Temple, a long-serving Jaguar man who preceded Andy Goss as president of Jaguar Land Rover North America, was certain that being British was a major selling point. He said that Ford of America's ownership was not a consideration for US buyers and neither was Tata's, although the takeover by the Indian company was viewed as positive: 'Our customers read the financial pages.'

Ratan Tata had instigated a specific focus on North America when he made a tour of US dealers soon after the JLR acquisition.

Jaguar dealers in the northern states told him that they were missing sales because they could not offer all-wheel drive. The subsequent fast development of the four-wheel drive XF and XJ was the first example of a new approach to overseas markets, tailoring products more closely to local requirements.

Other examples included offering a 3 litre petrol V6 and later a 2 litre four-cylinder petrol engine in the XJ for China, to fit local tax categories based on engine size. Closer to home, for the Dutch and Belgian markets, the 2.2 litre four-cylinder diesel in the XF was modified and its power output reduced to bring the CO_2 figure below a specific tax threshold.

JLR was encouraged to regard India as its 'second home market'. Assembly of Freelanders started at Tata Motors in Pune in May 2011 but sales began slowly. Even with the tax reduction for local production, Freelander is quite expensive in India and it is seen as less stylish than the cheaper Audi Q3 and BMW X1 – which are also assembled locally. Tata Motors' 2011/12 results show that JLR sold 2,274 cars in India, 800 of which were Freelanders. Indian Hotels, part of the Tata Group, showed corporate solidarity by buying a fleet of Jaguars as courtesy cars for VIP guests. Early in 2013, the Jaguar XF became the second JLR vehicle to be assembled in Pune.

Surprisingly, the Indians who buy premium cars do not seem to have a patriotic pride in Tata's ownership of JLR. But then perhaps that is just as well, as Tata cars have a poor reputation for reliability in the Indian motor trade.

Over the years, quality and reliability have also been big issues for Jaguar and Land Rover. Jaguar used to blame problems with its cars on the component suppliers, claiming that Jaguar's small volume of purchases compared with the volume marques meant that they didn't have the clout to demand the highest quality. It couldn't say that when it was part of Ford, which, in any case, had made a significant improvement in Jaguar build quality. At one time, the Land Rover Discovery was particularly noted for its propensity to break down. Again, outside suppliers were often blamed but it was clear that the build process at Solihull was in need of an overhaul.

Jaguar's quality and reliability improved further through the PAG era and since the Tata takeover it has consistently improved its position in the customer satisfaction surveys conducted by the respected research firm, J.D. Power, on both sides of the Atlantic. In 2012 in the US Initial Quality Survey it was named the most improved manufacturer, tying with Porsche for second place behind Toyota's Lexus brand; while in the 2012 UK survey of owners of 1–3-year-old cars, conducted by J.D. Power in conjunction with *What Car?* magazine, Jaguar was number one, toppling Lexus for the first time in 11 years.

But Land Rover remained among the back-runners in the same surveys. By the end of 2012 there were signs of improvement but the real test would come after a year or more of experience with the new products, made after the upgrades to the Solihull and Halewood plants.

Thanks to increased sales, and the popularity of the Evoque, the Land Rover franchise became highly rated by dealers. In 2012, *Motor Trader* magazine, representing UK dealers, nominated Land Rover 'Carmaker of the Year'.

With the integration of JLR manufacturing and sales, gaining an equally high reputation for both marques for quality and reliability of products and service from dealers became an important objective; in 2012, that was still some way from being achieved.

13

Enter the Evoque

ALTHOUGH LAND ROVER SALES had grown steadily through 2011, it was the Range Rover Evoque that really made the difference. The Evoque was the first vehicle to break the mould formed by the original Land Rover, 63 years before, and not only was it absolutely the right car at the right time for JLR but it also broadened the outlook for the Land Rover brand.

Here was a vehicle that would sell primarily on its appearance. Evoque looked good enough, and different enough, to appeal to buyers who previously would not have considered a Land Rover, while retaining the high seating position and promise of security, on and off the road, that had made SUVs so popular.

Global brand director, John Edwards, was sure that at least 80 per cent of Evoques would be conquest sales – replacing cars from rival manufacturers. There would be three- and five-door versions to suit different customer groups, one sporty, the other more practical. A palette of bright colours, including two-tone with a contrasting roof, and a wide variety of options and cosmetic enhancements, showed that it was aimed at Mini owners wanting to trade up to something bigger and smarter. (Interestingly, Mini sought to upstage Land Rover by launching its Countryman in the year before the Evoque). The styling was also expected to tempt owners of sports coupes like the Audi TT. The prestige of Range Rover lettering on the bonnet and tailgate was a final flourish.

So Evoque was not just a car or an SUV – it was a fashion item. There were no doubts about that from the day that the name was announced and it was previewed to a select media audience at Kensington Palace in London. The party, on 1 July 2010, coincided with the fortieth anniversary of the Range Rover, and was held in conjunction with *Vogue* magazine, which had first given its name to posh Range Rovers in the 1980s. There was a posh surprise when Spice Girl-turned-fashion-designer Victoria Beckham was nominated Range Rover's creative design consultant and appeared on stage with Gerry McGovern.

This caused some confusion as it was reported that Mrs Beckham had designed the Evoque, while actually at that time she had had no input (the £80,000 Victoria Beckham Limited Edition would appear two years later at the Beijing Motor Show). But her presence, and the fashion environment, gave Land Rover huge coverage in parts of the media that would not normally be interested in cars.

Of course, motoring publications knew the real story and were impressed by the way that McGovern and Land Rover exterior design manager, Jeremy Waterman, had evolved the LRX concept into the Evoque.

Not many pure concept cars make it to production without significant changes. Automotive historians point to rare examples like the first Audi TT, which came out of Volkswagen's advanced design studio in California, and the Isuzu Piazza, designed by the Italian maestro, Giorgetto Giugiaro. That McGovern's LRX concept survived with no more than a few millimetres added or taken off here and there, some extra air vents and other minor details, is a tribute to the attention paid to devising the original. McGovern was sure: 'You cannot show a concept and then deliver a pale imitation.' The company was determined to offer a genuine 'designer' product in the marketplace.

That determination made the engineers' job more difficult than anticipated. LRX was intended to share the underbody and mechanical units with the Freelander 2 but it soon became clear that a rethink of the chassis would be needed if it was to meet JLR's performance and fuel economy objectives and have the refinement and characteristics of a Range Rover. In the end, Evoque and Freelander had only one chassis component – a rear suspension mounting – in common. But the cars' basic layouts remained the same – transverse-engined front-wheel drive with a clutch system automatically engaging four-wheel drive when required.

Fashion plate or not, Land Rover's brand values required the Evoque to have the off-road capability of all its other products. But in the interests of fuel economy and lowering CO_2, it had decided to offer lower-powered Evoque and Freelander models with front-wheel drive only, like ordinary family saloons. The company gambled that the relatively small proportion of sales for these lighter and more frugal models would not damage its reputation for versatile, go-anywhere vehicles. Most of Land Rover's competitors already offered two- and four-wheel drive versions of their compact SUVs.

'Job 1', the start of Evoque production at Halewood, was exactly a year after the Kensington Palace preview. In the meantime, it took pride of place in the Land Rover displays at motor shows around the world, often accompanied by social events as a soft sell to the local 'lifestyle' media.

Orders flowed in, even though no potential customers had driven the car. Evoque already looked like a hit; by the time of the press launch in August, brand director John Edwards was confidently predicting that it would be Land Rover's best-seller. That would be good news, particularly if its sales were not at the expense of Freelander, which had been its most popular model. As a Range Rover, Evoque would be priced £6,000 above Freelander with the same engine, so there would be an immediate effect on the bottom line.

The driving preview for the press warrants mention here because of the bold exercise Land Rover staged to prove its abilities. The participants, from all over the world, found themselves on a remarkable adventure, which started in Wales, on an on- and off-road route following a water pipeline in Snowdonia – which in itself showed that the four-wheel drive Evoque was made of the right stuff – and led to Liverpool and a visit to the re-vamped Halewood plant. There was a diversion along the way, down an embankment and diving into a disused railway tunnel running 3 km under the heart of the city. It was pitch black within and for the last 100 metres the tunnel floor of ruts and rubble became a deep pool of water. The Evoques, lights ablaze, romped though it; those journalists who had been inclined to dismiss it as an urban 'soft-roader' were finally convinced that the Evoque was a true Land Rover.

By the time the first cars were delivered in September, the order bank was approaching 20,000. An extra 1,000 production workers had been taken on at Halewood but even with the plant working two shifts at full speed, there would be a delay in fulfilling those orders. Ralf Speth rejected calls to instal more capacity at this stage, knowing that, all too often, an initial surge of enthusiasm for a new model is followed quickly by a slump in demand. But early in the New Year, as the orders continued at an even greater pace and the Evoque received more and more favourable reviews, it was clear that production would have to be increased. Twelve months after the first car had left the production line, another 1,000 people were recruited at Halewood to enable the factory to run three shifts and operate on a 24-hour basis for the first time in its history.

At the end of the first year, 102,000 Evoques had been produced, which, in volume terms, was a record for any Land Rover model. Its first fashion item was well on the way to repaying the £500 million project cost. JLR had given Tata its first major hit.

Evoque won an array of 'best car' awards, made by magazines, journalist organisations, TV programmes and websites. Perhaps the most significant was North American Truck of the Year, an independent contest judged by 50 motoring writers from the US and Canada, presented at the January North American International Auto Show in Detroit. In America, the 'truck' class includes everything from massive crew-cab pickups to compact SUVs and MPVs. The list of recent NA Truck of the Year winners included blue-collar work trucks like the V8-engined Ford F150 and Chevrolet Silverado, but for 2012, the Evoque, a small British luxury crossover with a four-cylinder engine, took the honours.

The Evoque's win came as a shock to the US industry, for which Detroit is the home show. Apart from rewarding the Land Rover's combination of style and capability, it illustrated how far downsizing of cars and trucks had progressed in America.

Land Rover was not able immediately to capitalise on this success as, for the first time in many years, JLR did not exhibit at the Detroit show. The dates clashed with Auto Expo in Delhi to which, for obvious reasons, JLR felt obliged to take its latest products and concept cars. Ralf Speth flew from Delhi to Detroit to receive the NA Truck of the Year trophy but visitors who searched for Land Rover in its customary place in Detroit's Cobo Hall found Lincoln, Ford's sole remaining premium brand, displayed there instead. Some thought that was symbolic.

Back at Gaydon, Land Rover was already looking at ways of maintaining Evoque's momentum. In February 2012, ten days before the opening of the Geneva Motor Show, it invited a group of European motoring journalists to Pinewood film studios near London, where a number of Defenders were being prepared for their appearance in the opening action sequence of the James Bond film, *Skyfall*. But the visit was to reveal a top secret of a different kind: the Evoque Convertible.

Of course, there had been open-topped Land Rovers from the very beginning but the idea of a convertible version of a modern premium SUV was new (actually, not entirely, because a topless Nissan Murano had been launched in America – and named in a poll on the *AutoBlog* website as 'the most disliked car of 2011'). Most of those attending the Pinewood preview were surprised to see how well the Evoque survived losing its roof; the rising waistline of the three-door coupe helped it to look good, both open and with the soft top in place. The mechanism for the electrically operated fabric hood and the pop-up roll-over protection bars came directly from the Jaguar XK. Otherwise, the Evoque's mechanical specification was unchanged, so that the convertible could have the same off-road capability as the fixed-roof cars.

Whether the world needs a drop-top luxury off-roader is an open question but there was general agreement amongst the preview audience that the convertible would not look out of place in the sunshine of California and could appeal to the many female drivers in European cities who enjoy open-air Minis.

Although firmly labelled 'concept' when it was presented at the Geneva Motor Show, the Evoque Convertible was already earmarked for production; only the time and place had still to be decided. That decision wasn't imminent as JLR still had the problem that car manufacturers like to have (but say they don't): a backlog of orders for Evoque that would take several months to clear, even when Halewood was working at full capacity.

With Evoque exceeding all expectations, Land Rover brand management needed to concentrate on the replacement for the Defender, the successor to the rugged, go-anywhere vehicle that started it all. This had been the subject of a long and vigorous debate within the company. The Defender had recently been updated with a 2.2 litre diesel engine to comply with the latest Euro 5 exhaust emissions limits but a decision on a replacement would be needed soon as the current model would not meet new safety and emissions regulations to be imposed in 2016.

Technically, making a new Defender was easy; JLR had all kinds of four-wheel drive technology on the shelf and Land Rover benefited from more than 60 years' experience of building some of the toughest vehicles in the business. The difficulty was how to position the new vehicle – in price, function, comfort and style. Country people and rural public services remained loyal Defender customers but the military contracts had gone – armed forces now specified their own vehicles, usually comprehensively armoured – and in some countries it had become primarily a recreational vehicle for the affluent young.

Cool or tool? Could it be both? That was the question that the two DC100 concept cars were trying to answer when they first appeared at the 2011 Frankfurt Motor Show. DC100 stood simply for 'Defender Concept 100 inch wheelbase'. The sober grey fixed-roof two-door and the bright yellow open-topped Sport showed how a new modular design could provide different features for different applications. The surfers liked it but some of those who used the Defender as a workhorse were quick to declare DC100 unsuitable for purpose.

Although Land Rover described DC100 only as 'a potential future direction', the concept cars were displayed, dressed up in various ways, at several more motor shows through 2011 and 2012 and a few journalists were allowed 'test drives' (gently and at low speed, as they were styling models without proper running gear): the Sport on a beach near Los Angeles and the hardtop along a liner pier in New York harbour.

In an interview with the author in December 2012, Edwards said:

> We were genuinely interested in people's reaction to DC100 and there was a huge response – much of it very positive but some quite negative. We took some guidance from that and followed up with detailed research among the potential target market. It was the most extensive market research that Land Rover has ever done.

Although Land Rover's designers didn't need to go back to the drawing board (or, rather, the computer screen) to come up with a completely different idea, the project, code-named L660, went through several more iterations to arrive at the final design to be launched in mid-decade. Edwards hopes that this will please Defender enthusiasts but warns that they should not expect a direct replacement in the same image as the original: its market has changed and, in any case, the new vehicle must sell considerably more than the 16,000 Defenders produced in 2012.

By the summer of 2012, Land Rover was ready to present its other icon, the Range Rover, in a completely new form. With more performance, better fuel economy, greater comfort and the carbon footprint of a much smaller car, it was designed to satisfy both plutocrats and environmentalists. Described by Edwards as 'the gold standard of the SUV market', it represented Tata's largest investment in JLR so far.

14

Range Rover lightens up

THE RANGE ROVER, the brightest jewel in JLR's crown, was ready to make a big splash. It was a tense moment for the driver, David Sneath, the head of Land Rover events, as the car plunged into the pool and clambered over the rocks beneath. With water just below bonnet height, he had to feel his way forward to emerge precisely under the spotlights at the centre of the raised stage. His mission was accomplished: the all-new Range Rover had made a grand entrance while simultaneously showing why it is known as the king of the 4X4s.

The venue was suitably regal. White Lodge, an eighteenth-century mansion in Richmond Park on the outskirts of London, is a former royal residence; Queen Elizabeth II lived there as a child. Today, it houses the Royal Ballet School. Perhaps because the British royal family own and enjoy Land Rovers and Range Rovers, JLR was given the rare opportunity to take over the grounds of White Lodge to celebrate the launch of the all-new Range Rover.

A platform with a huge open-sided canopy was erected behind the lodge, overlooking the garden, and the giant rectangular pool with built-in rocks temporarily covered the normally immaculate 50-metre lawn. Five hundred guests, including media from all over the world, stars of sport and show business, and JLR's business associates, were treated to cocktails and canapés and, at the end of the evening, to an hour-long concert by Mark Knopfler.

An elaborate event like this is expensive to stage – exhibition specialists estimate that the Range Rover launch party cost well over £1 million – but was deemed essential to maintain prestige in the extravagant world of luxury products.

Bringing the new Range Rover to market had already cost a lot of money. It was Tata's largest single investment in JLR: about £1.3 billion, including £370 million to upgrade the Solihull plant with the facilities to make aluminium body/chassis units and a refitted paint shop.

The genesis of Project LR405 occurred during Richard Parry-Jones' time as chief technical officer of Ford. Regulations, environmental concerns and ever-rising fuel prices had made improving energy efficiency a high priority at Ford. The publication of official carbon dioxide (CO_2) figures made Land Rovers and Jaguars stand out as gas-guzzlers and, periodically, SUVs came under fire from consumer groups for being wastefully large and heavy for the everyday journeys on normal roads for which most were used.

The Range Rover not only claimed to be the most capable luxury 4X4 but was also an alternative to a conventional prestige saloon car. Reducing its size was not an option. Neither was fitting a puny, frugal engine. The only way to reduce its carbon footprint was to lose weight – and that meant aluminium body construction, as pioneered by Jaguar.

Under JLR engineering director Bob Joyce, body engineering is integrated, so Jaguar experience and expertise was applied to devise the largest aluminium stampings in the automotive industry – the new Range Rover's bodysides. These form the body/chassis frame with other pressed, extruded and cast aluminium components, using rivets and epoxy adhesive. On the new Range Rover production line at Solihull, octopus-arm robots that would have been welders instead quietly apply 3,722 rivets and 161 m of bonding to create each bodyshell.

Aluminium is much more expensive than steel and a large amount of power is needed to produce the prime material. Recycling not only makes full use of the aluminium but also requires only a fraction of the energy. Research based on the Jaguar experience allowed up to 50 per cent of recycled metal to be used in the Range Rover. Recycled aluminium is not suitable for all of the structure but the engineers joke that, if it was, a complete car body would need 28,000 soft drink cans.

The Range Rover's finished body weighs 180 kg less than the steel structure of the previous model, which means that it can use a smaller engine to give the same performance with better fuel economy and achieve a remarkable overall weight-saving of 420 kg – equal to five big adults. The result is a reduction in average fuel consumption (and CO_2 output) of up to 22 per cent.

With the spectre of legislation requiring a 25 per cent cut in CO_2 across JLR, making this major engineering change was essential. In the future, aluminium will be used for other models in the range. The next was to be the new Range Rover Sport, unveiled at the New York Auto Show in March 2013. The aluminium body facility at Solihull – the largest in the automotive world – has an initial capacity of 60,000 a year but can be expanded to 100,000.

Whether Range Rover customers care about energy saving is another matter. Global brand director, John Edwards, admitted that devising a new Range Rover, however it was made, was 'an interesting challenge'. Informal market research, conducted in all the major markets, elicited the universal response: don't change it, just make it better. Jaguar had the same reassuring reaction from its public before it introduced X350, the first aluminium XJ, but buyers subsequently drifted elsewhere. Edwards had no such worries: he was confident that his customers would remain loyal to the original Range Rover idea.

Gerry McGovern and his design team had the task of preserving that idea while at the same time bringing it up to date. McGovern said that the 2002 Range Rover was 'peerless' and that they had to be 'very mindful not to dilute that DNA'.

McGovern does not lack self-confidence. As an intriguing aside, he declared that Land Rover's is not a democratic design process ('democracy equals mediocrity') and was keen to acknowledge Ratan Tata's input: 'He is very design-literate and has been involved from the start. He nurtured and helped but never interfered.'

To the untrained eye, the new Range Rover doesn't look very different from the old but, in fact, it is longer and lower and changed in every detail; the only external items shared with the old car are the wheel nuts. The smoother, curvier front, with headlights like expensive camera lenses, presents a new face to the world and the redesigned interior provides more space and comfort for the occupants.

At the start of the project, the engineers identified an astonishing 175,000 different targets for this vehicle to achieve. Many were set well beyond previous JLR products; for example, the benchmark for running refinement (quietness and smoothness) was the Bentley Continental Flying Spur.

The test programme involved 300 prototypes and 800 component-testing rigs. Prototype testing took place in the frozen Arctic and in searing desert heat, from mountain goat-tracks to treacherous sand, and included 5,000 miles on the Nürburgring circuit in Germany, where the world's fastest sports cars prove their performance. In addition, JLR engineers estimate that its total of 1.5 million hours of CAE (computer-aided engineering) saved 750,000 miles of further on- and off-road testing.

A diesel-electric hybrid version of the new Range Rover was developed along with the conventional petrol- and diesel-engined models and scheduled to go on sale later in 2013. The hybrid system's electric motor is integrated with the automatic transmission and the batteries and control system are hidden under the floor, so nothing is lost in passenger accommodation or luggage space and the car's all-terrain capability is undiminished. The Range Rover Hybrid reinforces JLR's commitment to improving efficiency and reducing emissions; it offers the same performance as the top-of-the-range V8 diesel with an official CO_2 figure below 170 g/km.

The hybrid system adds another dimension to what is already one of the world's most technically complex cars; as launched, the Range Rover has no less than 64 separate ECUs (electronic control units, or on-board computers).

None of this comes cheap. There is no doubt that the world's first aluminium SUV costs significantly more to produce than an equivalent steel-bodied car so it was a surprise when Edwards announced that the price of what the industry calls the 'entry model' would be less than 2 per cent more than the previous Range Rover (£71,295 in the UK). That was a shrewd move because Edwards knew that the majority of Range Rover customers will go for more expensive versions and personalise their cars with the wide selection of extra-cost options, from two-tone paintwork to a 29-speaker premium audio system. A run of 500 of the extravagantly equipped Autobiography Ultimate Edition of the previous Range Rover had quickly sold out, despite – or perhaps because of – its exalted £120,000 price. A sizeable proportion of the new model was expected to sell for over £100,000, placing Range Rover firmly in the Bentley market – and ensuring a good profit for JLR.

The new Range Rover made its public debut at Mondial de l'Automobile, the Paris Motor Show, in September 2012. JLR had a large stand in a prominent position in the Porte de Versailles exhibition centre. This was a unique occasion as it was the first showing of the replacements for two automotive icons. The Range Rover to the right of the stand was balanced by the Jaguar F-Type on the left. They were both, by popular consensus, stars of the show. But there was no doubt which attracted the biggest crowd – and it wasn't the Range Rover. An SUV, however luxurious and technically advanced, is never going to have the pulling power of a two-seater Jaguar convertible.

Ratan Tata and Ravi Kant, on hand for the presentations on the show's preview day, could take satisfaction from the reaction to Tata's two biggest product investments, the way the two brands complemented one another and how the JLR plan, which they had agreed four and a half years before, had met its targets.

15

New ways for Jaguar

JAGUAR'S RENAISSANCE may have been made complete with the arrival of the new XJ, but it still wasn't selling many cars. In the 12 months to April 2012 the total for three models was 54,000, just 2 per cent more than the previous year and well below the 65,000 in Tata's first year of ownership.

It was true that it no longer had the X-Type, which had once been the biggest seller, and that its revenue per car had risen markedly with the new models, but by all measures Jaguar lagged way behind its companion brand.

When Adrian Hallmark was appointed Jaguar global brand director in December 2010, he arrived at Gaydon to find JLR management struggling with Jaguar's positioning. There was the dilemma about volume and price: should it follow Audi, BMW and Mercedes into small and relatively inexpensive cars or gradually move further upmarket with high-priced (and high-profit) low-volume models? And could it sip the cup of youth and finally cast off its image as the car that only your father buys by emphasising power and performance and perhaps making a return to motor racing?

As a dyed-in-the-wool marketing man, Hallmark realised that his first task was to analyse what Jaguar meant in the world outside the company. Surveys of 'brand health' suggested that Jaguar was in better shape than he had imagined; its power and recognition matched Porsche. Hallmark concluded that the marque's heritage, its sports cars and their success in racing, was still important but Jaguar's slogans of recent times – 'gorgeous' and 'beautiful fast cars' – didn't convey the right image in 2010.

Of course, compared with Audi, BMW and Mercedes, Jaguar was a niche player – but it wasn't always well equipped to fill its chosen niches. Tata was keen for Jaguar to spread its wings but didn't have limitless resources. As the new boy, Hallmark could see no reason why, in the long run, with the right investment, Jaguar could not move towards a million cars a year, like Audi and BMW. But for the present, he would have to concentrate on filling gaps in the current range to satisfy the changing demands of customers. He called this 'strengthening the voice of the market'.

Hallmark was well qualified for this job, having been managing director of Porsche UK, sales director of Bentley, in charge of Volkswagen sales in Asia – and, most recently, sales chief in the small team that tried to revive Saab after it was abandoned by General Motors. There are some ironies here: GM had looked upon Saab as its equivalent of Jaguar – and took its original shareholding on the rebound from losing Jaguar to Ford in 1989. The small Dutch sports car maker Spyker acquired Saab using loans guaranteed by the Swedish government at the same time as Tata was being rebuffed by the UK government but while Saab ultimately failed, JLR emerged stronger and fitter.

Coming to Jaguar two and a half years after the Tata takeover, Hallmark found that the course had been set for the next new model introductions: already under development were four-wheel drive versions of the XF and XJ, an XF estate car, and the two-seater sports car that would become the F-Type.

These new products would start to fill the gaps and were more precisely targeted than Jaguars of the past. The XF estate car, inexplicably named Sportbrake, was unveiled at the Geneva Motor Show in March 2012, eight months ahead of its on-sale date. It was only for Europe, where estate cars account for 20 per cent of the XF's market sector, and available only with four-cylinder and V6 diesel engines (more than 50 per cent of the market is diesel).

Ratan Tata had identified a demand for four-wheel drive Jaguars on his first tour of JLR dealers in the United States. Dealers in the northern snowbelt states explained that, as Jaguar's German competitors all offered four-wheel drive, their customers now expected premium cars to have all-weather capability.

So the four-wheel drive XF and XJ were primarily for the cold regions of North America and would be available only in combination with the latest supercharged 3 litre V6 petrol engine (diesel is not a factor in the US passenger car market). Appropriately, the Jaguar All Wheel Drive (AWD) models were first presented in a snowdome, specially constructed in Manhattan (albeit on a hot day in August). This was followed by a launch at the Moscow Motor Show; as well as living with freezing winter weather, Russian buyers favoured petrol engines.

These new variants and a wider engine choice – which included tax-reducing four-cylinder petrol engines for China – meant that, between them, XF and XJ competed in 80 per cent of the global luxury saloon market, compared with just 20 per cent four years earlier. The 2.2 litre four-cylinder diesel had already given the XF a boost. Global sales of 29,000 cars for the first six months of 2012 showed Jaguar was moving in the right direction.

The F-Type was different – not so much about increasing sales as creating a new spirit for the Jaguar brand. Hallmark is passionate about the F-Type. In an interview with the author in November 2012, he explained:

> It gets back to the meaning of the brand. Jaguar has a sports car history that most companies would die for but it didn't have a sports car in its range. Imagine Porsche without a 911 – it's unthinkable. The F-Type is the essence of the brand represented in physical form. With it, everything else makes sense.

At that time, everything else included C-X75, the F-Type's exotic brother. Heralded as 'the most advanced supercar ever conceived' when Hallmark announced that it was heading for production in May 2011, it was being developed with Williams F1, the Grand Prix car constructor, as a plug-in hybrid featuring a purpose-built lightweight and ultra-powerful (500 horsepower) 1.6 litre four-cylinder engine working in conjunction with two electric motors and a huge battery pack built into a race car-like carbon-fibre chassis. It promised the acceleration of a Bugatti Veyron – the world's fastest production car – and the exhaust emissions of a Toyota Prius. A small number would be made – 200 maximum – with an indicative price of £700,000.

Five running prototypes were near to the final specification when, in the first week of December 2012, the JLR executive committee decided to cancel C-X75. Hallmark said that it 'didn't feel comfortable launching a million-dollar supercar at a time of austerity'. Jaguar had evidence that some of the competition was struggling – a shaded reference to reports of slow sales for the forthcoming Porsche 918 hybrid – and concluded that the C-X75 would not make an adequate return on investment.

Hallmark put on a brave face to announce the first reversal of a product programme since Tata had acquired JLR. He said that the work on C-X75 would not go to waste: JLR's engineers had learnt valuable lessons on hybrid technology, aerodynamics and composite materials that would be applied to mainstream Jaguars.

'Performance hybrids' had a definite place in Jaguar's future line-up. The C-X16 show car had illustrated one approach to providing the liveliness of a sports car with fuel efficiency and CO_2 reduction that could ease both running costs and conscience. Enthusiasts loved the red 'push to pass' button on the steering wheel rim, intended to give the supercharged petrol engine an electric boost like the KERS (kinetic energy recovery system) of a Formula 1 race car.

Before it became involved with the C-X75, Williams F1 had worked with JLR in a Technology Strategy Board research project to create a hybrid Range Rover using a flywheel KERS but subsequent JLR hybrid development had concentrated on integrating an electric motor with the eight-speed automatic transmission used by both Jaguar and Land Rover. The first production application of this hybrid system would be with a diesel engine in a 2013 Range Rover but Jaguar will also use it, with the electronic control system differently calibrated to give the required 'performance feel'.

Like most other car companies, both JLR marques accept that they must offer hybrids to meet legislative requirements and future customer demand. But neither Jaguar nor Land Rover know how strong that demand will be. Such are the complexities of today's motoring world.

Jaguar was still the weaker of the two brands but, with a sales-man's confidence, Hallmark said that meant that it had more scope for growth. Speaking in November 2012, he pointed out areas ripe for expansion:

> Jaguar has 16 per cent of the premium car market in the UK, 5 per cent in the US, and everywhere else we are below 3 per cent. So there is huge potential. There is everything to play for in China – and in India, our second home market.

Long term, Jaguar's growth can only come with more new prod-ucts. The emphasis up to that time had been on increasing the number of variants of each model, so that Jaguar could cover more of the market. The next step would be to introduce addi-tional, fundamentally new models, but the debate continued about the best way to proceed.

Management was known to be split on the priorities for the allocation of funds. Was this the right moment to go for volume or would it be better to rebuild Jaguar's reputation for sporting and luxury cars and concentrate on making more money from each car sold? Readers will know that this is not a new question; successive managements have grappled with it since the 1980s.

In 2012, the modular (aluminium) platforms and engines in the JLR future programme provided many opportunities, including, for Jaguar, what has been described as 'an interesting and unusual take' on the idea of a four-wheel drive cross-over vehicle. It has to be different, because Ralf Speth has wisely decreed that Jaguar should never have an authentic SUV – and that Land Rover will never offer anything like a conventional saloon.

The design of a new, smaller Jaguar to compete with the BMW 3 series was ready in 2011 but since this car would require a heavy investment in production facilities – and engines from the new Wolverhampton plant – its introduction was delayed.

The F-Type was created at relatively low cost, mostly using existing components. After its launch in Paris in September 2012, it embarked on a world tour of the big motor shows: from Paris to Los Angeles, where on the eve of the Auto Show it was feted at a star-studded event at Paramount Studios, and thence to Guangzhou, Detroit and Geneva, ahead of its sales launch in April 2013.

The F-Type's job is to bring a youthful sparkle to Jaguar. It has been supported by an innovative marketing campaign devised with Spark44, a joint venture advertising and media agency brought together specifically for Jaguar. Instead of the anodyne 'Beautiful fast cars', the messages were sharper, more aggressive. One read: 'We have a finite number of heartbeats: don't waste them', alongside an image of an F-Type cornering at the limit on a blissfully empty winding road.

Jaguar believed that it had something to shout about: its first true sports car since the E-Type.

16

The F-Type saga

THE JAGUAR E-TYPE, the star of the 1961 Geneva Motor Show, was launched in the low-key style typical of the period. Sir William Lyons, the chairman of Jaguar Cars, sent an engraved invitation card to a small number of motoring writers to attend a press conference to introduce the E-Type at the Restaurant des Eaux-Vives, in a park overlooking Lake Geneva, at 4.30 in the afternoon on the eve of the show's opening.

By all accounts, the press conference was not much more than a photo-call and an opportunity to chat to Sir William and Bill Heynes, Jaguar's chief engineer, but immediately afterwards and throughout the motor show, journalists and prospective customers were given the opportunity to experience the E-Type on a short route in the hills behind the restaurant.

On 28 February 2011, to celebrate the fiftieth anniversary of this event, Jaguar went back to the Restaurant des Eaux-Vives with a collection of 20 classic E-Types and a lucky few successors to those senior motoring correspondents received an email invitation to join a re-enactment of the car's introduction.

Appropriately, Ratan Tata was there and took a ride in 77RW, the original E-Type demonstrator, with Carl-Peter Forster at the wheel. At dinner that evening, Norman Dewis, Lyons' chief test driver, bright and enthusiastic at 90, regaled the audience with the story of driving 77RW at astonishing speed through the night to reach Geneva in time to start the test runs. His account, like the car itself and the surrounding roads – open country 50 years ago and now lined with residences – illustrated just how much times had changed.

In an atmosphere heavy with nostalgia, the main topic of conversation between dinner guests was: why doesn't Jaguar have a car like the E-Type today?

When interviewed at takeover time, Ratan Tata said that he hoped Tata-owned Jaguar would produce a proper successor to the E-Type. He cited the Porsche 911 as an example of how to keep an iconic design of the 1960s fresh and relevant. At the Geneva dinner, the author reminded him of those comments. He replied wistfully, glancing at a beautiful original E-Type: 'We have a new sports car. I have seen it but it is not like that.'

There were good reasons for not making a retro car with the svelte fuselage shape of an E-Type. A drive in a bright red 1963 Series 1 coupe pointed to some of them: the car is narrow and the cockpit is cramped and, while it gave a more comfortable ride than today's sports cars, the braking and cornering grip provided by the skinny tyres on narrow wire wheels were woefully deficient by modern standards.

Ian Callum, Jaguar design chief, is a great admirer of the E-Type but explained that it was not possible for a car of its proportions and delicate detail to meet current and anticipated safety regulations. Everything from inner crush structures to driver's visibility and pedestrian protection would add bulk and threaten the purity of line. The E-Type's only passive safety features were seat belts.

Carl-Peter Forster and Ralf Speth had both acquired early E-Types since joining JLR but they didn't want to build a new one. Forster said: 'I am not a fan of looking backwards. We love Jaguar's heritage but society has changed in 50 years and we must build cars that cater for today's requirements.' Asked whether the new sports car being developed would show obvious E-Type connections, Speth replied: 'Please, not...'

Jaguar was careful not to make too close a connection between the E-Type – the fastest Jaguar of its time – and the XKR-S launched at the 2011 Geneva Motor Show. The 186 mph XKR-S was the most powerful version of the aluminium XK and the fastest production Jaguar ever made. Although Jaguar people were sworn to secrecy, it was known that the new two-seater would be based on the XK and, as it would be smaller and lighter, promised even higher performance.

Six months later, at Europe's biggest motor show in Frankfurt, Jaguar was ready to show its intentions. On a raised turntable at one end of the JLR stand was C-X16, a two-seater coupe which just happened to be exactly the same length as the first E-Type coupe and had the same kind of hatchback with a side-hinged door.

Motor show concept cars fall into two categories: either a radical new idea presented to gauge the reaction of the press and public, or a thinly disguised preview of a production model soon to be launched. C-X16 was the latter – a way of acclimatising the world to a new shape of Jaguar sports car that would be available in 2013.

C-X16 – the name said simply that it was Jaguar's sixteenth concept car – had a novel hybrid powertrain, which combined a 3 litre supercharged V6 petrol engine with an electric motor, arranged to provide an extra boost of power at the touch of a button. The first production version would be a convertible rather than a coupe, featuring the new V6 engine but without the hybrid elements.

Jaguar had set the scene but executives refused to be drawn on what the new car would be called. For the first time in recent memory, it presented a sports car without mentioning the E-Type. Ian Callum described C-X16 as: 'Our compelling vision for a 21st-century sports car, which embodies the established Jaguar strengths of sensual design, animal-like agility and inspirational performance.'

Behind the scenes, there was an intense debate on whether it should be called F-Type. The car had to be seen as something new and not a belated follow-on to the E-Type, but there were obvious marketing possibilities for a link with one of the most famous cars of all time. And for some of the longer-serving Jaguar people, the name F-Type was associated with failure. They had seen three before – and not one had made it to production.

The saga of the F-Type is worth a diversion, if only as an illustration of the changing fortunes and priorities at Jaguar under its previous owners. The first one, a project known as XJ41, was developed intermittently during the Egan years. What started as a relatively simple concept based on the XJ-S grew in power and complexity, and when, in 1990, it was cancelled by Bill Hayden, Ford's first Jaguar managing director, it was described as 'too heavy, too costly and too late'. The prototype passed to JaguarSport, run by Tom Walkinshaw's TWR racing operation, and was absorbed into the TWR project that became the Aston Martin DB7.

At Jaguar, the idea of an F-Type never really went away. In 1998, the XK180 was unveiled at the Paris Motor Show. A restyled and racier XKR, the 180 was intended to demonstrate how an uncompromised high-performance Jaguar could look. XK180 was never planned for production but it refocused on the sports car issue. 'But if we are to introduce another sports car it won't be like this,' said Jaguar's bosses. 'It will need to be a smaller and cheaper car to compete with the Porsche Boxster.'

Such a car appeared just 18 months later, at the Detroit Auto Show. The F-Type concept was the star of the show, a dazzling roadster that resembled a scaled-down XK180. Unusually for Jaguar, this was not a complete, running car but the idea was that it should be front-engined with rear-wheel drive and be powered by the 3 litre V6 from the S-Type saloon. Aware that the Porsche Boxster and 911 had some 40 per cent common components, Wolfgang Reitzle, president of the newly formed Premier Automotive Group, envisaged the F-Type sharing a chassis platform with a small, mid-engined Aston Martin.

A year later, at the Los Angeles Auto Show, Reitzle announced that Jaguar would develop the F-Type for production and that it would be on sale in 2004.

Back at base, the F-Type was presenting some problems. Ulrich Bez, the new head of Aston Martin, didn't want a mid-engined car and was keen for Aston to develop its own technology, and Ian Callum was having difficulty adapting the beautifully pro-portioned concept to the S-Type chassis. There then followed a trawl around the Ford world for an alternative rear-wheel drive platform – a bigger Mazda MX-5 was considered, as was cutting down the then-current (steel-bodied) XK. Eventually it was decided that it would share components with the X-Type, using a unique aluminium chassis with the saloon's transverse engine and gearbox installed amidships, driving the rear wheels.

This Project X600, mid-engined like the Porsche Boxster, became the third iteration of the F-Type. It was never shown in public, although some spy pictures and computer-simulated images appeared in the motoring press. Reitzle was pleased with this solution and could not disguise his enthusiasm when interviewed early in 2002:

> The F-Type is a unique, uncompromised, super Jaguar, which will surprise you, as it is different from what most people expect. It will be head-on with the Boxster in performance, price … everything. Porsche can't have this sector of the market to themselves forever.

But Porsche was going to continue to have a clear run. By June 2002, Reitzle had gone and Ford imposed new strictures on investment. X600, which was well on the way to production, was cancelled.

That might have been the end of the F-Type story but for the arrival of Adrian Hallmark as Jaguar global brand director in 2010. A smaller, two-seater version of the XK, code-named X152, was in the JLR product plan adopted by Tata. Hallmark had worked for Porsche and knew the sports car market. He also knew that the Boxster was so firmly established, and now surrounded by similarly priced competitors, that a small Jaguar was unlikely to add large numbers to JLR's sales and profits. But, he argued: 'A true sports car best expresses Jaguar. It will build the image, shining a light on the rest of the range.'

Hallmark commissioned market research in four countries (the UK, the US, Germany and China) to judge acceptance of X152 and an optimum price and specification. Further focus groups concentrated on possible names and 'F-Type' received wide approval. Based on those results, Hallmark thought it would be crazy not to capitalise on Jaguar's heritage and make the connection with its most celebrated model.

The United States had always been the main market for Jaguar sports cars. As we have noted, JLR didn't attend the official North American International Auto Show in Detroit in January 2012 but put on a big display in New York in April. The annual New York Auto Show, held in the Jacob Javits Center on Manhattan's west side, does not command the same attention as Detroit from the US manufacturers but is visited by larger numbers of the kind of people who buy Jaguars.

At the JLR press conference on preview day, the throng of reporters, photographers and TV crews saw a video of racing driver and TV commentator, Martin Brundle, putting a camouflaged open two-seater through its paces on the Gaydon track and heard Hallmark's announcement: 'This car, the most exciting product in Jaguar's modern history, is the next logical step in the sports car lineage – C-Type, D-Type, E-Type... F-Type!'

The real car wasn't in New York and wouldn't be seen in public undisguised until the autumn Paris Motor Show, still some months ahead of its mid-2013 on-sale date. In the meantime, the public was directed to a dedicated F-Type website and enthusiasts attending the Goodwood Festival of Speed saw the prototype, still camouflaged with a pattern of 'f's in all shapes and sizes, make a fast run up the hill-climb course driven by Mike Cross, JLR's car handling maestro.

In the following weeks a few more details were released. As expected, the engines to be fitted were the new Jaguar 3 litre V6 and the 5 litre V8 from which it was derived, and both would be supercharged.

In today's world of 24/7 news, manufacturers have difficulty managing information – in print, online and video – in the gap between the announcement and availability of a new model. Jaguar's communications staff handled the roll-out of the F-Type with skill, holding back pictures until just a few days before the launch in Paris. This was particularly important as the 2012 Paris Show would also see the debut of the all-new Range Rover, which would go on sale earlier than the Jaguar and was, in financial terms, much more important to JLR. They could not let the F-Type steal the Range Rover's thunder.

The Range Rover launch event was held in London three weeks before the official 'reveal' of the F-Type in the grounds of the Musée Rodin in Paris on the eve of the motor show. This was another lavish affair, with an audience of 500 dotted with celebrities. The American singer and songwriter Lana Del Rey performed 'Burning Desire', a song specially composed for the occasion, against a backdrop of the Jaguar sports car lineage from SS100, XK120, C-Type, D-Type, to E-Type – and pouring rain. A very damp Ian Callum took the opportunity to emphasise: 'This is not a latter-day E-Type. The F-Type has its own character, its own time, its own place.'

Selected journalists had already been briefed about the new car in confidential sessions at a hidden location in the Berkshire countryside, an ultra-modern private house which Jaguar had rented for the purpose. There, they had seen, heard and examined the car and learnt that it represented the fourth generation of Jaguar's aluminium body construction; the chassis was similar to but simpler and stiffer than the XKR-S; it was smaller and lighter; and the emphasis was on performance and driving pleasure: essential elements of a genuine sports car.

Hallmark said that the F-Type would be in a unique position in the marketplace, straddling the gap between the compact and 'full-size' two-seaters. Inevitably, he made a comparison with Porsche, announcing the F-Type pricing (starting at £58,500 in the UK) as midway between the Boxster and the 911 convertible: 'No one else offers the same size and performance at that price.'

So there had been a shift from Jaguar's long-held dream to compete head-on with the Porsche Boxster. By using existing components rather than developing a completely new car, it had been able to bring the new F-Type to production quickly and with relatively modest investment. It could be sold profitably in low volume – around 10,000 a year – and would revive Jaguar's reputation for proper sports cars.

What of the name? Hallmark was sure: 'We don't have to explain why we are making the F-Type. People will ask only, why haven't we done it before?'

17

Record profits

A NY REMAINING DOUBTS that Jaguar Land Rover was on the right track were dispelled by Ravi Kant, vice chairman of Tata Motors, when he gave a speech at the Geneva Motor Show in March 2010. He said not only had the market turned for JLR but, in the previous quarter, it had made more money than the rest of Tata Motors.

When the results for the year ending 31 March 2010 were published, JLR's full-year profit was a modest £51 million, reflecting the difficult conditions through most of 2009. But it was a turning point. Thereafter, profits improved consistently quarter-on-quarter – and by a substantial amount. By the autumn of 2010, the financial world had woken up and realised that JLR was heading for a full-year profit of more than £1 billion.

In three years, Tata had achieved a truly impressive turnround. In the first ten months of its ownership, JLR lost £376 million (and Tata Motors as a whole lost £370 million in the financial year 2008/9, mostly as a result of the acquisition). The profit before tax for 2009/10 amounted to just 0.8 per cent of revenue but in the following year had jumped to 11.3 per cent – which put its profit margin among the highest of any car company in the world.

Tata Motors and the Tata Group had kept JLR alive in the darkest days of the credit crisis but now JLR could be financially self-contained. In February 2010 it was able to take up the £340 million loan from the European Investment Bank (EIB), which had been bogged down in the murky dealings with the UK government the year before. This eight-year loan was granted under the European Clean Transport Facility and was specifically to finance the development of hybrid power units and energy-efficient, lightweight car bodies. Tata arranged guarantee support with Credit Suisse, which involved banks in India, the US and Germany, and declared that the EIB loan was the last major element in the funding plan to strengthen JLR's balance sheet. After that, it was on its own.

When JLR's £1.15 billion pre-tax profit for 2010/11 was announced, it was sitting on £1 billion cash. In May 2011, JLR was able to raise a further £1 billion through a bond issue, listed on the Euro MTF (multilateral trading facility) market; £250 million of the proceeds went to repay funding from Tata Motors, £380 million was used to repay other debt and £370 million was retained for future use.

In December 2011, the company put in place a three- and five-year £600 million revolving credit facility – later increased to £710 million – to provide standby liquidity, and in March 2012 issued a further £500 million bond through the Euro MTF market. By then, its cash reserves were up to £2.4 billion, with undrawn facilities of £849 million. It was, financial analysts agreed, in a very healthy position.

First of the new generation of Jaguars was the XF, launched in 2008 just as the Tata takeover was in process.

The new XJ appeared in June 2009 and, according to design chief Ian Callum, best represents the new face of Jaguar.

David Smith, a Ford finance man, was appointed JLR chief executive when Tata took control.

Carl-Peter Forster, ex-BMW and GM, was JLR chairman from February 2010 to September 2011.

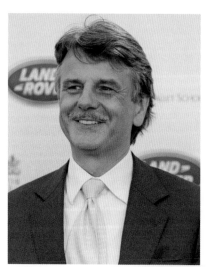

Ralf Speth returned to JLR as chief executive at the same time as Forster's appointment.

Phil Popham, previously head of Land Rover, has the job of integrating global sales for JLR.

Ian Callum, in charge of Jaguar design since 1999, showed a new way with XF and XJ.

Gerry McGovern, celebrated design chief of Land Rover, created the Evoque.

Jaguar director Adrian Hallmark was with Porsche and Bentley.

Land Rover brand director John Edwards came up through Rover.

JLR's greatest hit – the Range Rover Evoque is the fastest seller in the company's history.

Land Rover proved the Evoque's off-road capability with a test route through an abandoned tunnel under Liverpool.

Victoria Beckham positioned Evoque as a fashion item, launching her own version in Beijing, April 2012.

Supercar curtailed – Jaguar C-X75 demonstrated in Los Angeles, 2011.

DC100 concept of Defender replacement exercised on a New York pier, 2012.

JLR's 2012 show stars – Jaguar F-Type and Range Rover.

Four generations of Range Rover maintain the character recognised the world over. Forty-two years separate the Mark 1 and the latest model.

Robots at the Solihull plant apply rivets and adhesive rather than welds to build the all-aluminium bodyshell of the 2013 Range Rover.

Making a splash – the new Range Rover emerged from a rock-strewn pool to take centre stage at the launch party in Richmond Park, near London.

Living sculpture – the equivalent event for the Jaguar F-Type was held in the grounds of the Musée Rodin, on the eve of the Paris Motor Show.

Ralf Speth and Yin Tongyao, chief executive of Chery, at the ceremony to lay the cornerstone of the joint venture Chery Jaguar Land Rover Automotive Company, Changshu, China, November 2012.

Happy family – from the left, Cyrus Mistry, new chairman of Tata; Ralf Speth, Ian Callum, Ratan Tata, Gerry McGovern, Ravi Kant.

Ralf Speth could afford to be upbeat when he spoke at a press meeting in April 2012: '2011 is the year that changed people's perception of Jaguar Land Rover. It made £1 billion last year and £559 million in the last quarter alone, so we now have a sustainable, profitable business which is ready to expand like never before.'

The results covering the year up to 31 March 2012 confirmed the continuing upward trend. JLR made £1.507 billion pre-tax profit (from revenue of £13.512 billion) and was confident of continued growth through the following year. It paid a £150 million dividend to Tata Motors for the first time.

The first investment in the JLR expansion plan would be in people. Maintaining its new model programme and increasing long-range research and development required more engineers. Carl-Peter Forster had announced in June 2010 that JLR wanted to recruit 1,700 extra engineers but the right people were proving hard to find. Forster said that not enough engineers were being trained in the British education system and called for government support on issues related to skills and education. He warned that some JLR recruits, particularly electronics and software specialists, would have to come from overseas, including India. The aim was to build up the R&D headcount to 5,000 over five years.

Speth encouraged engineering links with suppliers and universities, and allocated a £100 million budget to extend the JLR advanced engineering team that was part of the Warwick Manufacturing Group (WMG) at Warwick University, conveniently close to Whitley. JLR would enlarge its core staff of 300 at WMG. TMETC, the Tata Motors European Technical Centre, is next door and also has about 300 people (the Tata Vista EV and the Pixel city car concept were developed there).

In total, JLR recruited 8,000 new employees between 2010 and 2012. These included 2,500 at Halewood (where there were 30,000 applications for one tranche of 1,000 jobs), 1,100 at Castle

Bromwich and 1,000 at Solihull – all to cope with increased demand for its products. Its annual graduate intake was increased to 330.

By the end of 2012, with both Halewood and Solihull working three shifts, JLR employed some 24,000 people in the UK – three times more than any other motor manufacturer in Britain. In January 2013, it announced the recruitment of 800 more staff at Solihull, initially on one-year contracts.

JLR could claim to make a significant contribution to the UK economy: £7 billion a year in gross value added (GVA) and, as one of the country's largest exporters, sold goods overseas worth £8.2 billion in 2011.

It was no wonder that UK politicians, once so reluctant to engage with the motor industry, were eager to bathe in JLR's success. David Cameron, prime minister in the Conservative–Liberal Democrat coalition government, deputy prime minister Nick Clegg, business secretary Vince Cable and a succession of junior ministers popped up at JLR's plants at every opportunity.

Government ministers see JLR's decision to build an engine factory in the UK Midlands as a real coup. At a time when the European motor industry is suffering from chronic over-capacity and even JLR's premium rivals are reducing costs by sharing engine production with volume manufacturers, a new engine plant is a rare thing.

Car body designs usually last for only one model cycle, six to ten years, but engines stay in production much longer – typically, for at least three generations of models. So as well as promising to invest £355 million and create 750 new jobs in the West Midlands, the establishment of an engine plant confirmed JLR's commitment to the UK.*

---

* In March 2013, JLR announced that it had scaled up their investment in the engine plant to more than £500 million and would increase recruitment to 1,400.

The plan and the location were discussed with the government in advance of the formal announcement made during a visit to Solihull by Nick Clegg and Vince Cable on 19 September 2011. A site at i54 South Staffordshire, a business park near Wolverhampton, was chosen because it was favourable for JLR's logistics and, as one of the government's new enterprise zones, qualifies for a regional growth grant of up to £10 million. Plant construction started in June 2012.

Making engines is also part of JLR's Chinese venture. After prolonged negotiations with possible partners and the Chinese authorities, in March 2012, JLR was able to announce that it had reached agreement with the Chery Automobile Company to form an equal partnership company that would make cars and engines for Jaguar, Land Rover and a new joint venture brand, and build a research and development centre in China.

Chery was founded in 1997, which makes it one of the longest-established of China's indigenous car manufacturers. With sales of 643,000 vehicles, it was the sixth-largest Chinese car company in 2011. Chery, which claims to be China's foremost vehicle exporter, had tried and failed with two previous international alliances – with Chrysler and Fiat – but this joint venture was on a much larger scale. It would involve a total investment of 10.9 billion RMB (£1.1 billion).

On 18 November, after the Chinese government had given the necessary regulatory approvals, the principals of the newly formed Chery Jaguar Land Rover Automotive Company laid the foundation stone for a new manufacturing plant in Changshu, near Shanghai. The factory, scheduled for completion in 2014, was expected to start production with the smaller Land Rover models, powered by JLR's new four-cylinder engines. The planned capacity, for all three marques, is 130,000 cars a year. All the vehicles made there will be for sale in China, which in 2012 overtook the UK to become JLR's biggest market.

Back in the UK, JLR management needed to reassure the workforce that the Chinese production would be incremental and no threat to their plants and jobs. On 30 October, as the formal approval for the Chery deal was posted on the official Chinese website, every employee received a letter or an email from Ralf Speth explaining the company's strategy.

Unite, the largest trade union represented at JLR, sounded a note of caution, despite having just accepted a deal that involved a pay increase of at least 7.5 per cent over two years and included a guarantee for the operation of all UK plants until 2022.

Although not directly connected to JLR and Tata Motors, Tata Steel was having a torrid time. With European demand for steel 25 per cent lower than before the recession and still going down, in November 2012, Tata Steel announced it was to cut 900 jobs and consolidate its 16 production facilities in the UK. The JLR unions noted that, when it had to, Tata did not shy away from tough decisions.

Outsiders continued to marvel at JLR's speed of expansion and the extent of its investment. For Tata, the tables had turned, and while JLR was making more than £1.5 billion profit, Tata Motors was struggling in its domestic market. Rising interest rates and fuel taxes in India – and an ageing model range – had caused a drop in Tata car sales of nearly 10 per cent in the first quarter of the financial year 2012/13.

JLR's success maintained Tata's confidence. In 2011/12, JLR generated nearly two-thirds of Tata Motors' revenue and more than 70 per cent of its pre-tax profit. By the end of the second quarter of 2012/13, that percentage was up to 90 per cent.

Analysing the results, *Bloomberg News* noted that JLR's planned expenditure of £1.5 billion a year for five years was more than the profit made by Tata Motors in 2011/12. That could be a warning sign for the future but for the time being the financial community regarded Tata as a good investment. Tata Motors was the second-best performing motor manufacturer stock in the first nine months of 2012; the share price had risen by 60 per cent, the biggest improvement on the Mumbai stock exchange.

At that point, Bloomberg calculated that Jaguar Land Rover was worth $14 billion. Tata's bosses had to smile: when it had paid $2.3 billion four years before, sceptical investors couldn't wait to offload Tata Motors stock.

18

JLR's place in the world

Shortly after the sale of Jaguar Land Rover to Tata, Ford chief executive Alan Mulally was asked if he thought that, at some time in the future, Ford would need to develop or acquire another premium car brand. His answer was a very definite no: 'All the premium brands together account for only 6 per cent of car sales worldwide.'

Mulally was being true to the principle established by Henry Ford, the company's founder: Ford's place was to build everyday cars for everyday people. The global volume of upmarket models is small beer when your main business is in multimillions. But, on the other hand, a premium brand has the undeniable attraction of promising a high profit per car sold.

That is, if it is done right. Not many of the 'generalist' car makers have succeeded in running premium brands. Ford was no exception. Over the years, it has become clear that it is more difficult for a maker of simple, inexpensive cars to establish a place in or near the luxury segment than it is for a premium brand to challenge the mass-producers.

The definitions are becoming blurred. Whilst there are a few well-recognised 'ultra-luxury' and 'hypercars' made in small numbers and sold at astronomically high prices, the mere 'luxury' brands in the price band below are gradually merging with those labelled as 'premium'. They, in turn, find themselves being challenged from the upper end of the generalists' model ranges.

Premium cars are the equivalent of airlines' business class. First class is represented by marques like Rolls-Royce, Bentley, Ferrari and Aston Martin; economy class includes all the mass-market cars that most people drive. In between, in price, specification and appointments, come the premium brands.

Jaguar anticipated the premium car as we know it today. The compact 2.4, 3.4 and 3.8 litre Jaguar Mk 2 saloons of the 1960s combined sportiness with features from traditional luxury cars and were offered at prices 30 per cent higher than mainstream models of equivalent size and type.

Others claim that Mercedes-Benz forged this middle sector of the market by eschewing smaller cars and concentrating on a range of solidly built, medium and large saloons with some of the style and prestige of the grand pre-war limousines that carried the three-pointed star.

It says a lot for the reputation of Mercedes-Benz – which goes back to the early days of the motor car – that it became one of the most admired premium car brands at the same time as being Germany's foremost supplier of workaday taxis, trucks and buses.

If Mercedes grew into the position of a premium car maker, BMW reinvented itself to become one. BMW started with a version of the British Austin Seven and produced the epochal 328 sports car in the 1930s – the car that is credited as the inspiration for the Jaguar XK120 – but after the Second World War found itself primarily a maker of motorcycles and economy 'bubble cars'. In 1962, after the Quandt family had rescued it from near-bankruptcy and the threat of takeover by Mercedes, BMW took the bold step of introducing the Neue Klasse 1500, a thoroughly modern, sharply styled mid-sized car that was the forerunner of the 02 and 3 series, the defining sports saloons of the 1970s.

While Jaguar concentrated on larger cars with bigger engines, BMW, with its more compact models, now brought the same qualities to a wider audience. In a fast-growing German economy, they appealed to the status-conscious 'executive' class: BMW became known as the 'businessman's express'.

Eberhard von Kuenheim, chairman of BMW from 1970 to 1993, can be seen as the most successful European car company leader of the post-war era. His strategy was to have interrelated models in three sizes – the 3, 5 and 7 series – all with a family resemblance and the same dynamic, sporty driving character. This would be the template for the many premium brands that followed, seeking a piece of BMW's success.

BMW's rapid progress – by 1972 its sales were over 100,000, and 30 years later they passed a million – can be attributed to strong, consistent leadership, allowing long-term planning and investment; high engineering standards; and, above all, a consistency of message. Its brand image – epitomised by the slogan 'the ultimate driving machine' – remains clear and is envied by manufacturers around the world.

The BMW brand was strong enough for the company's reputation to survive its disastrous sortie into Rover in the 1990s. The Rover debacle led to speculation that BMW was a takeover target but independence was sustained and it went on to make a success of its remaining British subsidiaries, Mini and Rolls-Royce Motors.

In those more extravagant times, the development of a big and powerful V12 engine for the 7 series was BMW's bid to match the world-respected technology of Mercedes-Benz. The Mercedes S-Class continued to rule at the top of the premium market but the brand with the three-pointed star was feeling pressure on its lesser models. It had introduced the 190 as a rival to the BMW 3 series in 1982 and, although it sold well, it was too conservative for most of the people who bought BMWs.

But it was Mercedes, rather than BMW, which drove the expansion of the premium sector. In 1993, the new chairman and chief executive, Helmut Wener, announced a radical plan: Mercedes would build a small front-wheel drive car (the A-Class), an SUV (the ML) and an MPV (the V-Class that became the Viano).

The battle that had been confined to traditional three-model ranges grew into a full-line confrontation. Suddenly there were no taboos – the premium brands could and would compete with the mass-producers by offering small cars, challenge 4X4 specialists like Land Rover, and even nudge into ultra-luxury and super-sports car territory. And now Mercedes and BMW were not alone.

Audi, under the technical guidance of Ferdinand Piëch (later to become supreme head of the Volkswagen Group), had come to prominence with two revolutionary cars: the 1980 Quattro, a high-performance sports coupe with four-wheel drive that became World Rally Champion, and the 1982 Audi 100, the first big saloon of its time to emphasise aerodynamic efficiency and weight reduction. A succession of new models followed, marketing and sales were separated from the Volkswagen brand, and Audi used the motto 'Vorsprung durch Technik' ('Progress through technology') to position itself alongside BMW and Mercedes.

Unlike the established premium players, Audi was part of a much larger car corporation. It was acquired by Volkswagen (ironically, from Daimler-Benz) in 1965 and shared systems, manufacturing, components and sometimes complete models with VW. So, although Audi had its own engineering and design departments and introduced many unique innovations, its rapid expansion through the 1990s and first decade of the twenty-first century was really an exercise in brand management.

Proof of that comes from within the Volkswagen Group. Piëch moved to Volkswagen in 1993 and to everyone's surprise initiated the development of the Phaeton, a large and luxurious saloon which shared most of its mechanical components with the Audi A8 and its W12 engine with the Bentley Continental. What was Volkswagen (literally, the 'people's car') doing, moving so far upmarket? Piëch explained: 'Mercedes is coming into Volkswagen's territory [with the A-Class], so Volkswagen will move into theirs.' Although built to the highest standards in a showpiece glass-walled factory in Dresden, the Phaeton didn't attract many buyers. It required too big a leap in price for traditional VW customers and had the wrong badge for those seeking the conferred status of a premium brand.

Other would-be premium brands had the obverse problem. Cadillac, America's most prestigious domestic nameplate, had shared the simple underpinnings of models from General Motors' other US brands for years but developed its own flamboyant style and features and had its own engines. In 1981, an ill-advised rationalisation within GM created a small car called Cimarron by Cadillac, simply by rebadging a contemporary four-cylinder Chevrolet. Some would say that Cadillac never really recovered. Certainly, it has never managed to make headway outside the United States

Lincoln and Mercury, linked divisions of Ford, were similarly inflicted with parts and platforms from regular Fords and it was inevitable that, when Ford started to take Jaguar seriously, it would seek economies of scale by sharing components with its higher-volume models. The S-Type, developed alongside the Lincoln LS, and the X-Type which was built on a Ford Mondeo platform, were not Jaguar's finest achievements.

As an aside, it is interesting to ponder why Jaguars related to less prestigious models were scorned, while there are few complaints about Audis that share platforms and complete component sets with Volkswagens, Seats and Skodas. Perhaps part of the answer is the Volkswagen Group's central planning, which ensures, more often than not, that the Audi version of a car on common platform is launched before the less expensive models. It may also be that Jaguar buyers care more passionately about such things.

The United States was the critical market for the development of premium brands. In the post-war boom, American motorists, disillusioned with cheap engineering and poor quality from Detroit, were eager to buy imported cars. Jaguar was popular but, like many other British cars, soon gathered a bad record for reliability. German cars – starting with the humble Volkswagen Beetle – were praised for their quality and durability. Mercedes, Porsche and BMW became the smart cars to own.

But by the end of the 1980s American car buyers had begun to resent what seemed like ever-increasing prices. For some years, fluctuating exchange rates had made import pricing problematical. Some of the Brits simply became uncompetitive and were withdrawn from the US, and Jaguar had looked vulnerable, but the Germans felt strong enough to keep adjusting prices upwards to preserve their margins.

Meanwhile, the Japanese manufacturers who displaced Volks-wagen as the provider of sound, inexpensive small cars saw the opportunity to make a quantum leap. Honda, Nissan and Toyota each devised a sub-brand, initially just for America, to sell upmarket cars larger in size and price than any of their previous offerings. Honda's Acura was the first to arrive but Infiniti (Nissan) and Lexus (Toyota) made a bigger impact when they were launched at the same time at the 1989 North American International Auto Show in Detroit. For the Germans, the Lexus LS400 and Infiniti Q45 were uncomfortably close in specification and presentation to the Mercedes S-Class and BMW 7 series – and priced 40 per cent lower.

It emerged later that Toyota had allocated an unlimited budget to produce its Mercedes rival and it was said that the Lexus LS was so expensively engineered that it would take ten years to pay back its development costs. It is not known if that first LS ever made a profit but Toyota achieved its objective: Lexus became the best-selling premium brand in America and stayed on top until BMW took the crown in 2011.

Lexus woke Mercedes up with a jolt, so that it cut prices in the US and accelerated plans to widen its model range. The LS was the flagship of a range of otherwise unexceptional models derived from Japanese-market Toyotas, which may be why Lexus found it hard to get established in other markets; it took 15 years to reach the 50,000-a-year critical mass in Europe. In recent times, Lexus has forged its own place among executive brands with a unique range of hybrids, for which Toyota is the technology leader.

Although it still doesn't have the worldwide reputation of the German marques, Lexus can be seen as a successful premium brand. But Infiniti and Acura have yet to fulfil their makers' hopes and expectations.

Infiniti was launched in Europe in 2008 as a kind of Japanese BMW, carrying the hopes of the Renault–Nissan alliance in the premium sector. One of the more surprising developments is a cooperative deal between Renault-Nissan and Mercedes, through which Infiniti receives Mercedes' diesel engines and is able to use the MFA chassis platform of the 2012 A-Class for a new model to be made at Nissan's UK plant in Sunderland.

Such collaboration underlines the extent to which the premium brands have ousted the generalists from the large and luxury car sectors. Until the 1990s, cars such as the Ford Scorpio, Opel Commodore, Renault Safrane and Citroen XM were steady sellers at the top of their respective ranges. Now, cars like this are actually or nearly extinct. There is a similar effect in the class below: in 2012, the BMW 3 series and Mercedes C-Class appeared in the UK car sales top 10 but the Ford Mondeo and Vauxhall Insignia did not.

While it owned Rover, BMW dithered about how to produce a successor to the Mini but when the new model finally appeared in 2001 (after BMW had cast Rover adrift) it single-handedly created a new market for premium small cars. Clever marketing played an important part: underneath the Mini's retro styling was a conventional small front-wheel drive car but an extensive range of attractive options provided opportunities for personalisation, making it something more special and able to demand a higher price than run-of-the-mill small cars.

Mini grew into a range of models (some far from mini-sized), which by 2012 had reached over 300,000 annual sales. Inevitably, there were imitators but they came mostly from the generalist manufacturers – the Fiat 500, Citroen DS and Opel Adam – which further blurred the premium boundaries.

The first of BMW's direct competitors to respond was Audi, which, because of its place within the Volkswagen Group, could quickly adapt the VW Polo to produce the A1. Mercedes' answer to Mini was the Smart brand but that tried and failed to widen its offer from the two-seater ForTwo city car; the ForFour and the Roadster and Coupe models were withdrawn after short production runs.

The next step was to bridge the gap. Audi already had an A3, which had become its best-seller. Mercedes needed a stronger contender in this category and gave up its gawky, upright A-Class design in favour of a sporty, coupe-like style, aimed squarely at BMW customers. It planned five different variants on this MFA platform. For its part, BMW concluded that it made sense for its smaller models to share a platform with the next generation of Mini; the first front-wheel drive BMW is scheduled for launch in 2014.

A regular stream of new cars has driven the expansion of the German premium brands and has given them the longest model lists in the industry. All three companies seek to fill every market niche and offer a car for every purpose. Their recent successes have been particularly with SUVs and 'crossovers': the Audi Q-series, BMW X Series and Mercedes ML – all of which are squarely in Land Rover territory.

The three German manufacturers have about 75 per cent of the global premium car business. In 2012, BMW led the pack with 1.842 million cars sold (1.54 million BMWs, the rest Minis and Rolls-Royces), Audi made 1.45 million, and Mercedes-Benz (including Smart and Maybach) made 1.42 million – the Mercedes brand alone made 1.32 million. By contrast, the record 2012 calendar year total for Jaguar and Land Rover was 357,000.

So Jaguar Land Rover has a lot of catching up to do. Not as much as Alfa Romeo, which BMW once regarded as its main rival, or Volvo, which has been struggling for years with its 'near premium' positioning, but it faces the widest-ever variety of rival products. JLR can't compete with all of them; one of its biggest challenges is to decide where to allocate resources for the most effective attack.

In 2013, it was clear that, in the car business, premium was the place to be. Of the mass-market car makers in Europe, only the Volkswagen Group was making progress – and Audi was its star performer. Ford, General Motors, Peugeot, Renault and Fiat were all poised to cut production and close factories. Premium brands, strong in territories that are insulated from the economic slowdown, bucked the trend. And analysts predicted they would enjoy a further 40 per cent increase in business over the next ten years.

19

Future unlimited

O N 10 DECEMBER 2012, Ralf Speth was waiting to check in for a flight to Riyadh. He was to brief a small group of motoring and motor industry writers in the Sofitel hotel adjacent to Terminal 5 at London Heathrow airport. Those attending, notebooks and recorders poised, had been told only that there would be major business news.

The news was good and bad. In the way of politicians, Jaguar Land Rover chose to link the announcement of an imminent deal with the Kingdom of Saudi Arabia, which should secure a supply of well-priced aluminium for its future cars, with the decision not to proceed with the C-X75 hybrid supercar.

The Saudi Arabian project was not a complete surprise. Three months earlier, interviewed by *Autocar India*, Ratan Tata had said that Tata was investigating the possibility of sourcing aluminium in Saudi Arabia and of setting up a plant there. He was a director of Alcoa, the US company that was building the world's largest aluminium production complex at Ras Al Khair in a joint venture with the Saudi Arabian Mining Company.

Speth was on his way to the formal signing of a letter of intent with Azzam Yaser Shalabi, the president of Saudi Arabia's national industrial clusters development programme, to pave the way for an automotive partnership for Saudi Arabia.

The plan being devised would supply aluminium sheet to JLR and also set up a press shop to produce finished aluminium components for Jaguars and Range Rovers.

Speth saw a guaranteed supply of aluminium as vital to secure JLR's future. Most of its future models would follow the Jaguar XJ, XK and Range Rover with lightweight aluminium construction. With the motor industry as a whole having to find ways of reducing vehicle weight, the demand for aluminium would increase rapidly in coming years and JLR, as a relatively small player, could be faced with a shortage or damaging price escalation.

Aluminium production is notorious for requiring huge amounts of energy. Saudi Arabia, with plentiful supplies of oil and gas, as well as bauxite, the necessary raw material, was well placed to provide aluminium of the right type and quality. The smelter would be in operation in 2014.

The second element of the partnership plan was to produce vehicles in Saudi Arabia for Middle Eastern markets. These would be designed and engineered by JLR, the initial product a Land Rover model that was not planned for the UK. Details were not disclosed, although obviously this car would have an aluminium structure. Reports from Saudi Arabia suggested that the plant could make 50,000 cars a year and require the partnership to invest $1.2 billion. It could be expanded to include Jaguar production in a second phase. Speth explained:

We are committed to further international partnerships to meet record demand for our vehicles. The Kingdom of Saudi Arabia is an attractive potential development option, complementing our existing facilities in Britain and manufacturing plans to expand in other countries including India and China.

The Chinese venture was already announced and the reference to expansion in India indicated that the Jaguar XF 2.2 diesel would join the Freelander 2 in its local assembly in Pune. JLR was also looking at the possibility of producing cars in Brazil. Import duties and local taxes made these overseas developments inevitable if JLR was to keep growing and profitably challenge the larger premium brands.

Speth is careful not to compare JLR directly with its German rivals. Although he announced in 2011 that it would launch 40 'significant product innovations' over the next five years, he stressed that JLR had different objectives: 'We are not chasing Audi, BMW and Mercedes volumes; we have our own strategy with more degrees of freedom, not just numbers. The big elephants do things differently; we are more pragmatic.'

Those significant innovations will include aluminium body/chassis for all but the smaller and more basic Land Rovers. The industry-wide drive to reduce fuel consumption and carbon emissions is unlikely to be reversed, even in better economic times. The same stimulus will bring a variety of hybrids and improved transmissions, including new and more efficient four-wheel drive systems.

JLR's Hotfire four-cylinder engines, to be built at the new plant in Wolverhampton, are key to its future. The current petrol V6 and V8 engines were designed at Jaguar and are exclusive to JLR but made by Ford at Bridgend in Wales, but the four-cylinder petrol and diesel engines are more or less to the same specification as those used in Ford's own vehicles. The new JLR engines can be tailored more precisely to its needs and there will be no contractual problems about producing them in China, India or elsewhere.

In the longer term, the larger V6 and V8 engines, petrol and diesel, will also need replacement. Jaguar has also worked its magic on the current diesels, although they also are supplied by Ford; the V6 comes from Dagenham but the 4.4 litre V8 for the Range Rover is made in Chihuahua, Mexico, alongside the engines for Ford's biggest pickup trucks.

Some industry pundits say that today's V8s are the last of a dying breed and that within a few years the most powerful versions of all but the most specialised sports cars will have smaller six- and four-cylinder engines. JLR keeps an open mind about that and has not declared how it will replace the large engines for which it is renowned. Since it seems certain that the number required will be reduced, the most likely scenario is to share with another manufacturer.

Given that there are established links between Tata and Fiat, sharing some engines with Fiat-owned Maserati seems a possibility. At the time of Tata's takeover of JLR, Fiat chief executive Sergio Marchionne said he would like to use the Jaguar XF platform for Maserati and Alfa Romeo but this could have contravened agreements with Ford; anyway, not long after, Fiat lost interest because it was joining forces with Chrysler.

The new four-cylinder engines are designed to be adaptable for transverse as well as longitudinal installation and are a pre-requisite for a small Jaguar, which is seen as essential for long-term success.

The premium car market is predicted to grow by more than 40 per cent over the next few years, with the biggest increases in the lower and higher price ranges. So as well as a small car,

Jaguar will venture further upmarket, re-employing the Daimler brand name, and both Jaguar and Land Rover will make more use of the ETO (engineered to order) department, which currently produces special editions like the Jaguar XJ Ultimate, XKR-S and the Victoria Beckham Range Rover Evoque. JLR's rivals have shown the popularity – and profit opportunity – of personalisation and there is plenty of scope for models specially trimmed and equipped for individual markets.

The success of the Evoque has emboldened Land Rover, which sees the prospect for a much wider range of vehicles in three categories: luxury (Range Rover), leisure (Discovery and Freelander) and dual purpose (Defender). Longer wheelbase and seven-seat versions of several models will be relatively easy to do and will be incremental sales. While Evoque evolves into a stylish family, including a convertible and a more luxurious model, there are plans for a series of utility vehicles to replace the Defender from a pickup truck to a capacious seven-seater-cum-load carrier.

JLR's first full hybrid, a version of the 2013 Range Rover, is something of an experiment. The company knows that it has to offer this technology – indeed, it believes that hybrids are the future for premium cars – but in the short term can only guess at the level of sales.

Most premium hybrids are aimed at the United States, providing an economical petrol-electric alternative to diesel engines, which hitherto have not been popular for passenger cars. The Range Rover Hybrid starts life as a diesel-electric, which effectively rules it out for America. A petrol-electric version will follow but if JLR's German competitors are successful in their drive to promote diesels in the US, it could be overtaken by the introduction of diesel Range Rovers there (a convergence of exhaust emissions regulations for Europe and the US should make that viable from 2016).

According to some predictions, by 2020 the global market for SUVs will be more than 20 million a year. If Land Rover can maintain a 3 per cent share, it will effectively double its 2012 production.

As well as opportunities, there could be obstacles ahead. It is possible to foresee the total production of JLR, from all sources, reaching 600,000 a year. Ironically, that could make the company more rather then less vulnerable, as it would come with an expensively developed model range more comparable to those of its rivals – who will still make twice as many cars.

JLR's success with its current range has not gone unnoticed, so other manufacturers will put extra effort into the market sectors where it has made the most progress. Range Rover's position as the most capable and luxurious SUV will be challenged as never before. The Volkswagen Group, bent on world domination – it expects to overtake Toyota and General Motors to become global number 1 by 2018 – is encouraging its premium brands to expand in this area. Between them, Bentley, Porsche, Audi and Lamborghini could offer tempting alternatives to each Range Rover model. Fiat has big plans for Maserati – an increase from 6,300 cars in 2011 to 50,000 by 2015 – with new models that are direct rivals for both Jaguar and Range Rover.

Jaguar may struggle to get a foothold in the intensely competitive market for smaller premium cars. With the big mass-producers nudging in with attractive 'near premium' offerings, it is increasingly difficult to find a profitable place among the ever-widening variety of small BMWs, Audis and Mercedes.

Under Tata's patronage, JLR 'overinvested' to make itself more competitive and was rewarded by three years of extraordinary profit growth. Financial analysts warn that JLR's 2012/13 profit may be a high-water mark and that, in the years to come, the many new ventures to which JLR is committed will drain its cash reserves.

As a wholly owned subsidiary, JLR's fortunes are directly linked to Tata Motors. By the end of 2012, as we have seen, JLR accounted for 90 per cent of its parent company's profit. Although JLR is fiercely – and rightly – protective of its brand values, in the long term there must surely be some technical crossover with Tata's own-brand products. In autumn 2012, Tata's car range was looking tired, and its sales were declining. This was the view of Bertrand D'souza, editor of India's *Overdrive* magazine: 'The cars now seem old fashioned, aesthetically and in touch and feel.' Tata in India was ready for an infusion of JLR's design and engineering skills.

Tata Motors also has to decide how far to venture into export markets with its Indian-built cars. By acquiring Jaguar and Land Rover, it automatically became part of the global car business and avoided the difficulty of launching an unknown brand in mature markets. Nevertheless, Ratan Tata held an ambition to sell a version of the Nano as the lowest-price new car in Europe and the United States. A decision on that will be taken by his successor.

Under Tata Sons rules, Ratan Tata retired on his seventy-fifth birthday, 28 December 2012. As the patriarch of corporate India, his are big shoes to fill. Anticipating his retirement, in 2010, the board of directors set up a committee of wise men from inside and outside the company – including Lord Bhattacharyya of Warwick University – to make a global search for his successor. The committee deliberated for 15 months before recommending 43-year-old Cyrus Mistry, already a director, whose family is a major shareholder in Tata Sons. The board elected Mistry deputy chairman in November 2011 and he would spend a year shadowing Ratan before taking over as chairman. He was appointed to the board of Tata Motors in May 2012.

Mistry is not from the Tata family but has close connections

– his sister is married to Noel Tata, Ratan's half-brother. He holds an Irish as well as an Indian passport (his mother was born in Dublin) and has strong ties with the UK: his education included a degree in civil engineering from Imperial College, London, and an MSc in management from London Business School.

Pallonji Mistry, Cyrus's father, is high on the list of Indian billionaires (worth $9.7 billion at the last count) and Cyrus was very successful in developing the family's construction and real estate group. Whether he will pursue expansion in the motor business with the same enthusiasm as Ratan Tata remains to be seen.

The motor industry is relentlessly expensive. New vehicles, new production facilities and long lead-times require constant investment. In India, financial commentators have questioned whether JLR and Tata would be willing and able to fund the kind of giant leap that would be needed to make JLR a full competitor for BMW. They have suggested that the time may come when Tata will sell a stake in JLR or float it on the stock market as a separate company, although there is no precedent for either course of action within the Tata Group.

Ratan Tata was asked about these possibilities by Graham Ruddick in a retirement interview published in *The Daily Telegraph* in December 2012, and replied:

> We have never said that we would not consider those things. We have nursed this company (JLR) as a 100 per cent subsidiary and I don't think we would be in such a great hurry to dilute ourselves. But, at the same time, if it's the right thing to do, we would consider it.

20

Why Tata succeeded

TATA TRANSFORMED JAGUAR LAND ROVER in its first five years of ownership. In 2008, the business faced an uncertain future. Ford couldn't wait to dispose of JLR, viewing it as a drain on resources that didn't fit within its enforced austerity strategy. Then, almost immediately, Tata was faced with the western world's worst economic crash of modern times and had to raise emergency funds to keep JLR afloat. But by 2011, JLR had returned an annual profit that wasn't far off the figure Tata had paid for the company.

A year later, JLR could claim to be among the most profitable car manufacturers in the world, with an operating margin of over 11 per cent. It had also made the largest investment in the UK motor industry in the twenty-first century.

The reasons that Tata succeeded can be summarised thus: it negotiated a good purchase price, committed the right investment, and applied good management. But, as this book has sought to explain, the scale of that success was determined by more subtle factors.

JLR is a car business: nothing more, nothing less. It generated the excellent profits that have made headlines by manufacturing and selling more of the cars that already existed or were being prepared for launch at the time of the Tata takeover. At the time there was much debate about whether Tata got good value for the $2.3 billion it paid Ford but the results have shown that, whatever else it inherited, it did receive an excellent range of products.

With the benefit of hindsight, it looks as if Ford overpaid when it bought Jaguar in 1989 and Land Rover in 2000, and then undersold to Tata. It was more or less a fire sale, and in the end Tata was the only vehicle manufacturer bidding. The Indians were able to make a good deal.

Ford may have anticipated the coming financial crisis – it was the only one of America's 'big three' car makers to avoid bankruptcy proceedings – but Tata certainly didn't expect a global meltdown less than three months after the JLR takeover. It took courage, and an industrial group with deep resources, to persevere with a plan for growth through the dark time that followed.

Because Ford didn't separate the members of its Premier Automotive Group in its published accounts, the outside world didn't know the financial situation of Jaguar and Land Rover at the time of the sale. Jaguar was reputed to carry heavy losses but Ford sources have since confirmed that JLR, as sold, was very profitable, thanks to Land Rover, whose vehicles were always among the best money-earners in the Ford empire. So, the turnround that Tata wrought at JLR may not be quite as dramatic as some have suggested.

Ford is known to be one of the better-run companies in the world's motor industry. JLR still benefits from the Ford product creation system, a series of disciplines to take a new car from concept design to the production line. Tata had no way of improving upon that and retained nearly all of JLR's existing engineering and manufacturing executives.

The 'hands off' strategy also applied to the administrative staff through the first two years of its ownership. After that, Tata began to bring in managers with a proven track record at other premium brands: both Carl-Peter Forster and Ralf Speth came, indirectly, from BMW; Adrian Hallmark had worked at Bentley and Porsche; Andy Goss, president of JLR North America, was from Porsche UK; and Jeremy Hicks, managing director of Jaguar Land Rover UK, had been responsible for the rapid expansion of Audi in Britain.

Tata encouraged JLR chief executive Ralf Speth to devise a new and leaner management structure to cut bureaucracy and speed up decision-making. Executives felt empowered as never before. One said: 'We were told to cut down the number of meetings and make them short. That never happened in the Ford days.' A seasoned Land Rover man welcomed the new stability: 'When we were part of BMW and Ford we felt like foster children, constantly being moved from one set of reluctant parents to another.'

Under Ford, Jaguar and Land Rover were distant subsidiaries for which all the big decisions were made by higher authorities at PAG, Ford of Europe and Ford World Headquarters in the US. Whilst JLR is wholly owned by Tata Motors, it is autonomous, sets its own strategy and handles its own finances. In other words, it has the freedom to be entrepreneurial.

A senior engineer described the new working atmosphere: 'Liberating. We have to live alone now, determine our own future. One immediate result was a much better relationship with suppliers.' This is no surprise to Lord Bhattacharyya of Warwick University, who championed the Tata takeover: 'There was no shortage of capable engineers at Jaguar and Land Rover. What was needed was capital, vision and leadership.'

Those are the things that have characterised Tata's ownership. Tata is ambitious and far-sighted and prepared to invest (or, rather, let JLR invest its earnings) for the long term. Several JLR managers have mentioned that Tata encourages them to be bold and think big, the opposite of an all-embracing corporation like Ford where the starting point of any project would be a tightly committed budget. This book has described the mind-changing and budget cuts that afflicted Jaguar and Land Rover as previous owners allocated resources elsewhere. Under Tata, once a project is agreed, it is for JLR to manage.

As well as developing and launching admired new products in a timely fashion, JLR has been judicious in the management of its factories, and keeping control of inventory – stocks of unsold cars are the bane of motor manufacturing. External factors dictated continuing with three UK plants, instead of two as had been planned, but when the demand for the new models was clear the workforce at all three was increased.

Tata has shown a clear understanding of how to make the business thrive. There are three ways for a car company to grow: increase market share, enter new market segments, and expand geographically into new markets. Over five years, JLR has either achieved, or is working towards, all of these and has done so simultaneously.

It is ironic that it took an Indian owner and German management to restore Jaguar and Land Rover's pride in being British. Soon after he arrived as chairman of JLR, Carl-Peter Forster reflected that 'the British don't always recognise their assets'.

In a premium car world dominated by three German brands, 'Britishness' was a positive marketing proposition and JLR took full advantage of Britain's excellent reputation in design, fashion and luxury goods. And it took a new pride in its heritage, encouraging a high-profile race series for classic Jaguars and showing the original Range Rover alongside its twenty-first century aluminium successor.

Combined sales for the two brands in the 2011/12 financial year were the highest ever – 314,433 wholesale – and heading for another leap forward in 2012/13.

Tata could have maintained JLR much as it had been through the previous decade, improved its efficiency and taken the profits back to India. It could have sold off Jaguar, and a number of commentators thought that it would, once the new Ford-developed products had been launched. Instead, it adopted – and expanded – an ambitious new plan proposed by JLR management.

The chosen path required a continuing hefty investment by JLR – more than £7.5 billion over five years, almost £3 billion in 2013 alone – as well as payback of the money that Tata raised to keep it going through the difficult first two years.

As with most business successes, a slice of luck accompanied Tata's good judgement in handling JLR. Sales of the Range Rover Evoque vastly exceeded the expectations of Land Rover's sales management – and even Tata's more optimistic estimates. As a smaller, more friendly SUV, the Evoque was the right car at the right time for a marque labelled 'gas guzzler' by environmentalists who, a couple of years before, had issued fake parking tickets to Range Rover owners stating 'Bad car choice!'.

In the UK, Land Rovers were also redeemed by two exceptionally hard winters; as someone said, it was a rare example of a motor vehicle benefiting from rather than being held responsible for climate change.

The Evoque's success worldwide, continuing strong growth in the SUV sector, and multiplying sales for both Land Rover and Jaguar in China are the most important factors underlying three years of increasingly strong earnings.

Without question, Tata made a successful acquisition in 2008. For its part, Tata never had any doubts, even during the worst of the financial crisis. Five years on, it is illuminating to see the confidence expressed by Ratan Tata in the chairman's statement for the Tata Motors 2009 annual report:

> I feel confident that if we can sustain our operations through this difficult period we could overcome all obstacles in our path. I feel strongly that in later years we will look on Jaguar Land Rover and say to ourselves that this was a very worthwhile strategic acquisition and one which brought us considerable technology and global presence.

Ratan Tata, retiring just short of the fifth anniversary of the JLR takeover, achieved his ambition: Tata Motors, with Jaguar Land Rover, really had become a car company of consequence.

Appendix

Key players

Personalities featured in this book who shaped
(and are shaping) Jaguar Land Rover

Lewis Booth (b. 1948), chairman and chief executive of Ford of Europe and the Premier Automotive Group, was chief negotiator in the sale of JLR. After the sale he moved to Dearborn, Michigan, to be Ford Motor Company chief financial officer. Started at British Leyland but had a 34-year career at Ford, including time in Asia and South Africa. He retired in 2012 and now lives in the US and the UK. He is a non-executive director of various companies, including Rolls-Royce PLC.

Ian Callum (b. 1954), design director of Jaguar, is one of the UK's most celebrated car designers. He has been head of design at Jaguar since 1999 but only in recent years has he been able to bring his vision for the brand to reality, with the revolutionary XF and latest XJ. He designed the beautiful Aston Martin DB7 and used to avoid any clash of style between Aston and Jaguar but no longer feels so constrained.

Bob Dover (b. 1948), is an engineer-manager who has been intimately involved with Land Rover and Jaguar through most of his career. He was manager of the Solihull plant, chief engineer on Discovery, and programme manager for the Jaguar XK8. A spell as managing director of Aston Martin was followed by a return to Land Rover, leading to the roles of chairman and chief executive of Jaguar and Land Rover. He retired from JLR in 2003 and now serves as a director of several engineering companies.

John Edwards (b. 1962), global brand director Land Rover, is a marketing specialist who came to Land Rover by way of Rover, which he had joined in 1990. Brand manager and then UK director of Mini and MG, he transferred to Land Rover when it was acquired by Ford. Appointed brand chief in December 2010 in time to oversee the two most important launches of JLR's Tata era: the Evoque and the 2013 Range Rover.

Sir John Egan (b. 1939), was brought in to take charge of Jaguar in 1980 by Sir Michael Edwardes, chairman of British Leyland, and turned a dysfunctional business into one that was successfully floated on the London stock exchange in 1984. Egan left in June 1990, six months after Ford purchased the company, and went on to a high-profile career as the managing director of the British Airports Authority. He was knighted in 1986.

Mark Fields (b. 1961), was chairman and chief executive of Ford's Premier Automotive Group from 2002 to 2005, latterly also head of Ford of Europe. He made his name as president of Mazda when it was run by Ford. Returned to his US home-land in 2005 to a job with the portentous title of President of the Americas. Appointed Ford chief operating officer in 2012, number 2 to chief executive, Alan Mulally.

Carl-Peter Forster (b. 1954), group chief executive of Tata Motors and chairman of JLR from February 2010. A German born in London, he was a board director of BMW but disagreed on the future of Rover, left and became chairman of General Motors Europe. Recruited to Tata after breakdown of sale of Opel. Left for personal reasons in September 2011. Non-executive direc-tor of various companies including, from January 2013, Geely Automotive, the Chinese owner of Volvo Cars.

Adrian Hallmark (b. 1962), global brand director, Jaguar, joined JLR in December 2010. Trained in engineering but career in sales and marketing: managing director of Porsche UK at the age of 34, became sales and marketing director of Bentley, fol-lowed by positions at Volkswagen in the US and Asia. In 2010 was part of the small group that attempted to revive Saab, when briefly owned by Spyker.

Bill Hayden (b. 1929) was chief executive of Jaguar Cars for less than three years but made his mark on the company by bring-ing Ford production processes to what had become a chaotic industrial scene. Hayden was about to retire as Ford's European vice president of manufacturing when he was put into Jaguar in 1990. He pulled no punches, calling it 'a terrible organisation making terrible cars' but by the time he left, in 1992, the basis for a more efficient future had been established.

Ravi Kant (b. 1944), managing director of Tata Motors at the time of the JLR acquisition, was the most prominent Tata representative during the takeover process. As Ratan Tata's closest lieutenant, he was influential in the reorganisation of JLR. Reached retirement age in 2009 and his place taken by Carl-Peter Forster. Appointed vice chairman in his retirement, Kant took back some of his old responsibilities when Forster left in 2011 and continues to play an important role.

Charles Spencer (Spen) King (1925–2010), was the father of the Range Rover. He joined Rover in 1945 and worked on its gas turbine cars before being appointed chief engineer. The Range Rover was a side project when Rover fell into British Leyland in 1968 and King became chief engineer of Rover-Triumph. Its enduring success was marked by a special 'CSK' edition for the twentieth anniversary and King, who retired from BL in 1985, had been planning to attend the car's fiftieth anniversary when he was taken ill following a bicycle accident and died at the age of 85.

Sir William Lyons (1901–1985), the proprietor of Jaguar Cars, which grew from the Swallow Sidecar Company he had founded with William Walmsley in 1922. Noted for his skill and discernment in car design, Lyons was a canny businessman, who made judicious purchases of complementary companies. In 1966 he merged Jaguar into British Motor Holdings, which became part of British Leyland. Lyons, who was knighted in 1956, retired in 1972 and was given the honorary title of president of Jaguar.

Gerry McGovern (b. 1956), design director, Land Rover, has been described as Britain's hottest car designer, following the success of the Range Rover Evoque. Came to prominence at

Rover with the design for the MG F sports car and the Land Rover Freelander, and was poached by Ford to head Lincoln-Mercury design in the US. Returned to Land Rover as director of advanced design and was appointed to the top design job in 2008.

Alan Mulally (b. 1945), was parachuted into Ford from Boeing, where he had headed the commercial aircraft division. Appointed chief executive in 2006 and immediately upset new colleagues by proclaiming that his Lexus LS430 was the best car in the world. Among his first decisions was to concentrate all efforts on 'One Ford', which would lead to the sale of Jaguar and Land Rover. Over five years achieved a remarkable company turnround in America, although Ford of Europe was still struggling.

Jacques (Jac) Nasser (b. 1947), was responsible for bringing Jaguar and Land Rover together in Ford's Premier Automotive Group in 2000. Earlier, as head of Ford automotive operations and then chief executive, he had promoted the expansion of Jaguar, turning it from a two- to a four-model range. Ousted from Ford in 2001; the company's finances were in decline and the board disagreed with his policy of diversification. From 2010, chairman of the Anglo-Australian BHP Billiton mining group.

Richard Parry-Jones (b. 1951), was chief technical officer at Ford in the latter days of the Premier Automotive Group. Re-organised PAG product development and initiated a fuel efficiency programme which included the aluminium Range Rover. Left Ford in 2007 and became an advisor to the UK government on policy in the auto and manufacturing sectors. From July 2012, chairman of Network Rail, responsible for UK railway infrastructure.

Geoff Polites (1947–2008), the incumbent chief executive of Jaguar and Land Rover at the time of the Tata takeover. An Australian, with experience of the retail motor trade, he headed Ford Australia before being transferred to Ford of Europe and joining PAG in 2005. Championed Ian Callum's new style for Jaguar and Gerry McGovern's Land Rover LRX that became the Evoque. Died in April 2008, before the Tata deal was finalised.

Phil Popham (b. 1965), Jaguar Land Rover director, global sales and service operations, is a Land Rover man through and through, joining as a graduate trainee in 1988 and rising through the ranks under three different company owners. Within PAG he was UK managing director of Jaguar and Land Rover and then global head of Land Rover. In the JLR reorganisation he took responsibility for integrating the sales operations of the two brands worldwide.

Wolfgang Reitzle (b. 1949), had a meteoric rise at BMW. Personal assistant to chairman Eberhard von Kuenheim, he took charge of BMW research and development in 1984 and was responsible for new models from the 1986 7 series. Chairman of Rover Group 1995, initiated the third-generation Range Rover. In 1999, left BMW, recruited by Ford to run new Premier Automotive Group (which launched his Range Rover). Left the motor industry in 2002 to be chief executive of Linde, the world's largest industrial gas company.

Sir Nick Scheele (b. 1944), headed Jaguar from 1992 to 1999, when he was appointed chairman Ford of Europe. In the wake of Jac Nasser's departure he became president of Ford Motor Company, alongside Bill Ford as chairman. Jaguar production trebled in Scheele's era, as Ford got to grips with quality and efficiency issues and sanctioned new models. A Brit with world-wide experience, Scheele was knighted for export achievements in 2001. He retired from Ford in 2005.

David Smith (b. 1961), was a finance executive at Ford of Europe when the call came asking him to return to Jaguar Land Rover (his previous job had been finance director of PAG) as chief executive-in-waiting. Geoff Polites died in April 2008 and Smith was formally appointed to the top job when the Tata takeover was completed in June. Only weeks later, he was faced with the economic crash and the downturn that followed. After a difficult 18 months, he left JLR and in July 2010 became CFO of British technology company, Edwards Vacuum.

Ralf Speth (b. 1955), was appointed chief executive of Jaguar Land Rover in February 2010. Spent 20 years with BMW, where his final appointment was vice president of Land Rover, transferred to PAG and became director of production, quality and product planning. Left to join Wolfgang Reitzle at Linde, where he was head of global operations. Returned to JLR in February 2010 as chief executive working with chairman Carl-Peter Forster. Has reorganised and streamlined JLR with direct reports from an 18-man executive committee.

Lord (Donald) Stokes (1914–2008), chairman of British Leyland from 1968 to 1975, presided over the amalgamation of most of the British motor industry, including Jaguar and Land Rover. Many future projects were cancelled in a rationalisation of the marques but the Range Rover survived as Stokes could see its export potential. He was given a life peerage in 1969 and took the title of Lord Stokes of Leyland, where he had made his name as export director for the eponymous trucks and buses.

He retired from business in 1980 and died in 2008 at the age of 94.

Ratan Tata (b. 1937), is the key to this success story. As chairman of Tata Sons and its associate company Tata Motors, he had the vision to purchase Jaguar Land Rover and give the Indian company a prestigious entrance to the world motor industry. Fascinated by car design and engineering, he has participated in the development of all JLR's new products as well as ensuring the financial health of the business. Stepped down as chairman when he reached the age of 75 in December 2012 and was named chairman emeritus.

Maurice Wilks (1904–1963), was the inventor of Land Rover, inspired by the need for a four-wheel drive vehicle for his own farm but also as a production opportunity for Rover in a time of post-war austerity. The younger of the two brothers who ran Rover; Maurice was chief engineer, Spencer, managing director. Worked with Gordon Bashford and, later, Spen King (his nephew) to develop the Land Rover, which first appeared in production form in 1948.

Mike Wright (b. 1953), executive director, Jaguar Land Rover, is the longest-serving employee on the JLR executive committee. Started out as graduate trainee at Rover-Triumph, had a succession of senior marketing jobs at Rover and Land Rover, then, under PAG, was UK managing director of Jaguar and Land Rover, and Jaguar Cars overall. Played a vital role in the preparations for the sale to Tata and the establishment of JLR as a stand-alone business.

Jaguar Land Rover financial performance

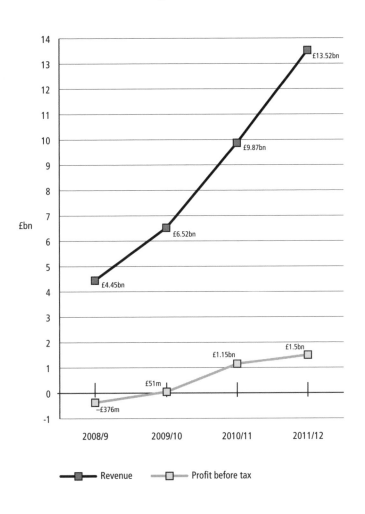

£bn

£13.52bn

£9.87bn

£6.52bn

£4.45bn

£1.5bn

£1.15bn

£51m

−£376m

14
13
12
11
10
9
8
7
6
5
4
3
2
1
0
-1

2008/9   2009/10   2010/11   2011/12

■ Revenue   □ Profit before tax

Jaguar Land Rover sales 2007–2012

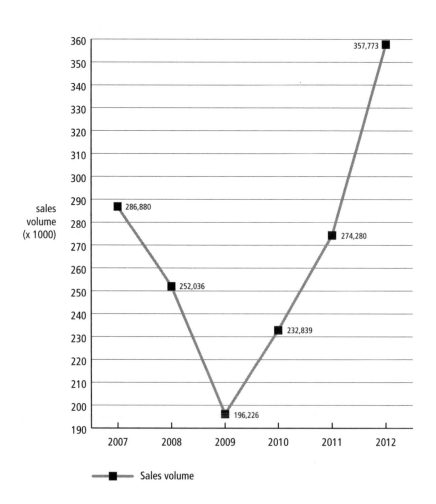

Marque sales year-by-year

	Jaguar	Land Rover
1948	4,251	8,000
1949	4,190	16,085
1950	7,206	17,360
1951	6,496	19,591
1952	8,968	18,570
1953	10,099	20,135
1954	9,894	28,882
1955	10,868	28,365
1956	13,205	25,775
1957	13,676	28,656
1958	19,456	28,371
1959	18,619	34,168
1960	23,352	35,148

	Jaguar	Land Rover
1961	25,224	37,139
1962	24,181	34,304
1963	23,923	42,569
1964	25,862	45,790
1965	26,905	47,941
1966	23,082	44,191
1967	21,961	44,928
1968	23,351	50,561
1969	28,614	47,624
1970	29,608	59,200
1971	31,549	57,955
1972	24,541	56,243
1973	27,893	53,773
1974	35,882	63,197
1975	21,752	60,721
1976	24,759	51,119
1977	23,507	57,412
1978	27,605	54,309
1979	14,283	60,906
1980	14,865	51,500
1981	14,093	52,181
1982	22,048	40,768
1983	28,041	37,447
1984	33,437	37,086
1985	37,745	33,689
1986	40,993	41,290
1987	46,643	46,250
1988	49,495	51,251

	Jaguar	Land Rover
1989	47,400	49,314
1990	42,753	58,370
1991	25,667	52,245
1992	22,499	56,886
1993	27,381	73,268
1994	30,102	90,050
1995	39,776	115,590
1996	39,019	125,222
1997	43,848	128,048
1998	50,225	153,495
1999	75,312	178,000
2000	90,031	169,492
2001	100,791	164,010
2002	130,332	174,593
2003	120,570	165,163
2004	118,918	162,422
2005	89,804	185,120
2006	75,013	192,511
2007	60,485	226,395
2008	65,446	186,590
2009	51,855	144,371
2010	51,444	181,395
2011	50,678	223,602
2012	53,847	303,926

The figures for Land Rover 1948–2012 and Jaguar from 1985 onwards are from JLR and refer to retail sales. Those for Jaguar 1948–1984, kindly supplied by Jaguar Heritage, are production volumes and therefore may differ from annual sales figures quoted elsewhere.

These are calendar year figures for comparison purposes. JLR adopted Tata's April–March financial year from 2009.

Premium brand league

Excluding brands that sell only models priced above £100,000

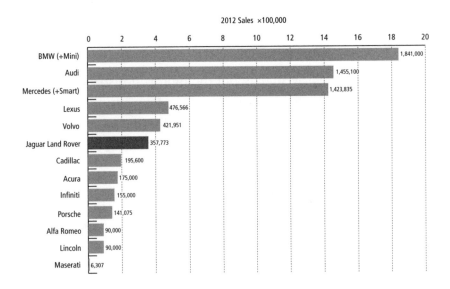

2012 Sales ×100,000

BMW (+Mini)	1,841,000
Audi	1,455,100
Mercedes (+Smart)	1,423,835
Lexus	476,566
Volvo	421,951
Jaguar Land Rover	357,773
Cadillac	195,600
Acura	175,000
Infiniti	155,000
Porsche	141,075
Alfa Romeo	90,000
Lincoln	90,000
Maserati	6,307

Acknowledgements

Of the many books written about the motor industry in general and Jaguar and Land Rover in particular, the author is pleased to acknowledge the special value of the following in the preparation of this work:

American Icon: Alan Mulally and the Fight to Save Ford Motor Company, Bryce G Hoffman, Crown Business 2012

The Beaulieu Encyclopedia of the Automobile Vols 1 & 2, Ed: Nick Georgano, The Stationery Office 2000

Comeback: The Fall and Rise of the American Automobile Industry, Paul Ingrassia and Joseph B White, Simon & Schuster 1994

The Complete Book of BMW, Tony Lewin, Motorbooks 2004

Jaguar, Lord Montagu of Beaulieu, Quiller Press 1990

Jaguar: Rebirth of a Legend, Ken Clayton, Century Hutchinson 1988

The Land Rover 1948–1988 Collector's Guide, James Taylor, MRP 1988

Rover: The First Ninety Years, Eric Dymock, Dove Publishing 1993

Range Rover: The Anniversary Guide, Mike Gould, Porter Press 2010

Autocar, Britain's oldest motoring journal, of which the author was once editor, is a consistent weekly source of information on the motor business and its products and was often used as reference.

Picture credits

The majority of the photographs in this book are from the files of Jaguar Land Rover and were taken by its official photographers. The publishers thank JLR and the following who also supplied images:

Autocar
British Motor Industry Heritage Trust
Giles Chapman
Roger Crathorne
Ford Motor Company
Ray Hutton
Jaguar Heritage
The Linde Group
Overdrive
Tata Motors
Alan Zafer

About the author

Ray Hutton has been writing about the motor industry and its products for more than 35 years.

He recalls that one of his first assignments as a fledgling motoring journalist was to attend the official unveiling of the original Jaguar XJ6 in London. A couple of years later, as sports editor of *Autocar* magazine, he was to use one of the first production Range Rovers to travel to motor races across Europe and cover rallies throughout the UK.

By the time that Jaguar and Land Rover came together in nationalised British Leyland, Ray had been appointed editor-in-chief of *Autocar*. In that capacity, he followed the progress of the two marques for nine years – and has been doing so ever since. Maintaining an overview of the business has involved travelling the world, interviewing captains of the motor industry, and assessing and reporting on their products.

Freelance since the mid 1980s, Ray writes on cars and the motor business in magazines, newspapers and websites worldwide, including *The Sunday Times*, *Motor Trader* (UK), *Car and Driver* (USA), and *Overdrive* (India). His previous books include *The Centenary History of the Fédération Internationale de l'Automobile (FIA)*, published in 2004.

Ray is honorary president of the international Car of the Year Jury, vice president of the UK Guild of Motoring Writers, and an associate member of the prestigious British Racing Drivers' Club. His work has won the Montagu Trophy awarded by the Guild of Motoring Writers and, on two occasions, the Bentley International Award.

A science graduate from Queen Mary, University of London, he lives in London with his wife Elizabeth.

Index

and Jaguar 10–13, 35, 36,
37–8, 41, 42–5, 59–60, 66,
80–2, 85, 122, 138–40,
158, 173
and Land Rover 22–3, 35,
38, 40, 59, 60–1, 122, 173
sale of Jaguar Land Rover
(JLR) vii, 2, 28, 48–54, 58,
65–6, 67, 171–2
see also Premier Automotive
Group (PAG)
Ford Motor Credit 67–8
Ford of Europe 10, 36, 41, 44,
45, 47, 55, 66, 173
Ford World Headquarters,
Dearborn 38, 43, 46, 54, 173
Formula 1 6, 28, 41, 131
Forster, Carl-Peter 22, 87–92,
93–4, 95–6, 99, 100–1, 105,
136, 137, 147, 173, 174, 181
Frankfurt Motor Shows 81,
101, 117–18
Freelander, Land Rover 31,
36–7, 38, 60, 82–3, 100,
103–4, 109, 113, 114, 165,
167
fuel economy 42, 43–4, 62, 70,
72, 113, 118–19, 122–4, 131

G

Gaydon technical centre 38,
40, 41, 47, 48, 50, 51, 53, 59,
63, 104, 116, 127, 141

Geely 49
General Motors 9, 10, 17, 20,
22, 36, 40–1, 49, 73, 85, 87,
88, 90, 128, 157, 162, 168
Geneva Motor Shows 1–4, 27,
87, 89, 117, 129, 135, 137,
145
Giugiaro, Giorgetto 113
Global Corporate Council 30
Goldman Sachs 45, 48
Goodwood Festival of Speed
141
Goss, Andy 107, 108, 173
government, British 7, 8, 9, 10,
20, 53, 69, 70, 72–3, 77–8,
85, 148–9
Green, Andy 90
Greenwell, Joe 44–5
Guy Motors 6

H

Halewood factory 13, 38, 59,
76, 82, 92, 94, 100, 103–4,
110, 113–14, 115, 147
Hallmark, Adrian 105, 127–33,
140, 142–3, 173, 181
Hams Hall factory (BMW) 22
Harriman, Sir George 7
Hayden, Bill 11–12, 138,
181
Heitmann, Heinrich 22
Heynes, Bill 135
Hicks, Jeremy 173